GREEN MONEY

GREEN MONEY

HOW YOUR MONEY CAN WORK HARDER FOR YOU AND SAVE THE PLANET

DAVID MACDONALD

First published in Great Britain in 2023

ISBN: 978-1-7393119-0-2 (paperback)
978-1-7393119-1-9 (ebook)

Published by:
Matthew's Gate Publishing

Design and production:
Catherine Williams, Chapter One Book Production

Cover design:
Daren Newman

CONTENTS

PART ONE

CHAPTER 1

YOU CAN SAVE THE PLANET ...

This book is really the story of how you can save the planet. That may sound like a grandiose claim, but I aim to convince you it's not. What I'm about to share with you is how you can use your money and influence to create the biggest impact and help avert the climate crisis. We are at a tipping point, where consumers are realising they can harness their power to effect the changes the planet and its people need. It's not just people but all earthlings that need a radical shift to take place.

Since you are reading this book, you may well be one of these early adopters and visionaries who will be the catalysts for this change, assuming you "buy" the concept. And I believe you should – it's my contention that it's one of the biggest win-win scenarios ever. Not only will you achieve a great sense of purpose and fulfilment from making this change, it will have financial rewards – as mass adoption accelerates investment in solutions and guides your investments away from dinosaur companies destined to fail.

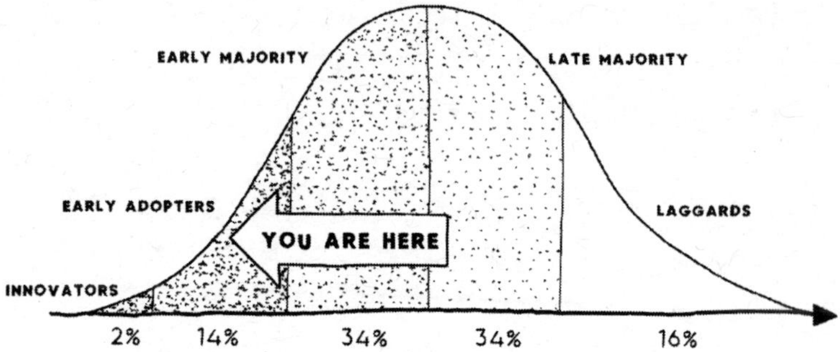

Figure 1: The Start of the "New Normal"

How it all started

Before we dive into the specifics, I want to tell you the story of how I got here, and how the company I founded, Path Financial, was created.

I started my financial services career in a head office at the Guardian Royal Exchange in Edinburgh's St Andrew Square. I quickly discovered that the salespeople in the organisation seemed to have more glamorous jobs than me. It transpired they had expense accounts, company cars and got to go to the pub on Friday afternoons. That was the life for me! And so, I requested a transfer to the London King William Street branch to move into sales. My request was flatly refused, and I was told, 'You will never make it in sales, Macdonald – get back to your desk and get on with your work.'

As a child of the Thatcher era, I decided to "get on my bike" and seek to fulfil my less-than-lofty hedonistic ambitions in London. Financial markets had recently been deregulated by the Financial Services Act and the Big Bang in 1986. With the obvious opportunities this would create, the lure of the Square Mile was too strong to resist. My first day did not dawn brightly, when a bird pooped on me on the way into the offices of my new employer (although apparently this is a sign of good luck). Maybe the bird knew something I didn't – as Black Monday followed shortly thereafter. That was the biggest one-day fall in financial markets, with many losing a quarter to a third of their values overnight.

In retrospect, starting out in the midst of the biggest financial crisis in most people's memories taught me resilience and tenacity. I learned the importance of establishing exemplary processes for well-diversified portfolios that could perform optimally. My first year in the business was spent working as a self-employed salesman with Save & Prosper. Then, because of the polarisation of the Financial Services Act, I moved to the other end of the spectrum as a broker consultant with Scottish Equitable. After a stint employed by a very large and trendy independent financial adviser (IFA) who went spectacularly bust, I switched to bancassurance with Royal Scottish Assurance (RSA). I saw all sides of the business, with very solid grounding and robust training and experience. From there, I started my self-employed career, joining a fledgling IFA with colleagues from RSA, which I ended up owning and then selling.

Around 2006, I moved my practice to St. James's Place, because they were a firm with what I felt was an exceptionally robust investment management process. (I still believe this and have the highest regard for them.) Their partners have great client relationships, and their ground-breaking investment management is still effective. Furthermore, the SJP Foundation does fabulous work for charity, though is sadly under-recognised for all the good it does. I still desperately miss the late and great Mike Wilson, co-founder and for many years Chief Executive of St. James's Place. He was one of the sweetest and kindest men I have ever met – a truly great businessman and a gentleman. He had a positive approach and with his customary twinkle in his eye, I felt he always got the best from people.

For much of my career I was taught to create "well-diversified investment portfolios" that made the maximum financial return and growth, which was all fine until I noticed that focusing purely on profit caused money to do bad things – or, more accurately – encouraged the people managing it to cut corners and find the fastest route to maximum profit, regardless of the cost and the consequences. (You may agree, dear reader, that we've reached the stage, as a people and a planet, where the motivation of "profit at any cost" is no longer fit for purpose and we need to do better. Better in every sense of the word.)

Around this time, I met my future wife, Tara (who is an absolute inspiration to me), and explained to her all about the process of financial planning and how to build an investment portfolio. She was rather dismissive. She remarked that "all I did was make rich people richer", and I thought, *well, uh, yes, but they're very appreciative*. I knew we were skilled at finding ways to help people identify their financial goals and then hit their objectives, but I was, as you might imagine, a bit put out by this. It sat at the back of my mind, and niggled away at me. Tara had quickly got to the nub of the issue. It occurred to me it wasn't perhaps the most purposeful use of a life, despite how much my clients appreciated it. It was an interesting comment – no one had ever said anything like that to me before – but I was happily building a successful practice, so I continued with business as usual.

My Netflix Epiphany

Some years later, I started hearing hard evidence of climate change. I was also doing a lot of work on exploring my most deeply held personal values since I felt some things were incongruent in my work and life. At a serendipitous point in this process, my eldest son, Ruairidh, urged me to watch a documentary on Netflix called *Cowspiracy*. Reframing farming, the programme illustrates the impact animal agriculture has on the environment, the huge amount of carbon emissions it creates, and how it causes more damage to the environment than the entire transportation industry. It came as a surprise to learn this harm wasn't being talked about or widely understood – not by me and not even by world-renowned environmental organisations. It was perturbing to realise that the investment funds I recommended to clients funded many of the companies mentioned in the film – not only animal agriculture but all the other polluters and those responsible for poor working practices. I learned that American actor and film producer Leonardo DiCaprio was the executive producer. DiCaprio is a vegan and a campaigner for large pension funds to disinvest from companies which have caused environmental harm and climate change. I immediately took an interest in this divestment movement, and the more I understood it, the more I saw that so many of the companies we were funding and investing in were creating a great deal of environmental and social harm – not to mention killing people, all earthlings and the planet. What else can you say about tobacco and oil companies and deforestation if not that?

This was a wake-up call for me – my work was deeply in conflict with what had emerged as one of my core values. I set about finding out more about the dramatic impact the divestment movement would have on companies if investors shunned the shares and sold them. It struck me that many companies might change their ways if their share prices were harmed by people moving their money out of harmful stocks and shares. By putting millions of pounds into these investments every year, I was part of the problem. My eyes had been opened to the way the markets and the capitalist process operate together. The only ethical choice I could make based on my moral position was to stop investing in the traditional way. No matter how inconvenient for me personally, I had to cease being part of the problem and quickly made the life-changing decision to sell my business and take early retirement.

I planned to use my newfound environmental conscience to do whatever I could for the planet, and in some positive way make amends for my behaviour of the preceding years. On reflection, I held somewhat of a whimsical vision of picking up plastic bottles off the beach while walking the dog to the sound of crashing waves. After a busy and challenging career, I had no idea what it would really be like to retire, but one immediate problem I faced was the proceeds from my business sale – once a financial planner, always a financial planner. I figured I'd better invest the money to create a functional retirement fund.

Investing in Solutions for the Planet

Having learned about divestment, the first step for me was to exclude certain companies I no longer wished to support. And on this illuminating journey, I learned of the emerging *impact investment* movement, which is about not only excluding companies but investing in companies which actively contribute towards solutions for the planet. And so, this was how I began tackling the thorny problem of where to invest my money. While the "screen out" of companies that didn't fit my new green criteria was relatively easy, the "screen in" was extremely difficult. I struggled to find anyone with a decent investment management process in the impact arena. And this was me as a seasoned professional with three decades of experience in constructing functional investment portfolios.

There is a whole "alphabet soup" of jargon in the green or ethical investment space. Definitions are thin on the ground and measurement is difficult. Investment is complex and boring enough, but it quite simply becomes extremely difficult when you try to pick out more virtuous investments from the morass of damaging ones.

A Gap in the Market

Eventually, I found two analysts who had considerable experience in the field and very strong processes. Neither process was particularly accessible to the ordinary retail investor. Considering how difficult it was for me as an experienced financial professional to make this transition, I discovered there was a gap in the market for financial advisers who specialised in positive impact investment only. I realised this had to be the way forward to empower consumers. Not only that, but financial returns would emerge as being stronger than traditional investment. An idea like this could surely influence the financial services and fund management industry to accelerate the move to a more caring capitalism. This thinking now seems to be much more accepted, but at the time – this was pre-Greta Thunberg's arrival in the global arena – it was seen as somewhat "crackpot". With more recent upswings in inputs into greener funds and a focus on finance at COP26 and COP27, despite the recent surge in oil prices due to the war in Ukraine, this is now an inevitable transition and a new mega-trend.

Around that time, I also learned about "stranded assets", which is the term associated with fossil fuels and oil companies no longer being allowed to release the same volume of carbon dioxide (CO2) into the atmosphere. Growing awareness of environmental concerns and the race to be carbon neutral means they will have to reduce or stop extracting hydrocarbons, which will impact their balance sheets dramatically. The value of these companies is too high, and when this change happens, they will plummet. And so, even from a pure investment perspective, I considered it a poor decision to be investing in that type of company for the long term.

In 2022, which I believe will be an anomaly, shares in oil and gas companies generally spiked, which inversely correlated with stock markets generally declining. This, in some considerable part, was due to the supply issues caused by the dependence on Russian oil and gas. This crisis has highlighted the danger of overdependence on fossil fuels. It really doesn't need to be this way. Renewables are more abundantly available and their price is at an all-time low. In fact, when you consider the wind, the tides and how much sun falls on the planet, there is limitless renewable energy to be had. It seems to me we will inexorably move to renewables reasonably quickly – a pace of change which investors can influence and no doubt profit from. It will be interesting to see if the *oil* companies realise they have to be *energy* companies in order to adapt, and how if they don't, they'll die.

Using Your Money for Good

It dawned on me that if you invest in emerging technologies that are trying to save the planet, there will potentially be above-average returns. If offered the choice to help save the planet rather than keep killing it with their investment, would people choose the former?

The Country's First Positive Impact Investment Financial Adviser

So, retirement didn't last long! I had an insight that my entire purpose in life was to take this newfound passion and bring it to market as the country's first positive impact investment financial adviser, empowering consumers to make a choice in helping address the climate crisis. What a fantastic and refreshing opportunity! I had the luxury of putting the investment process together with a completely clean sheet and some financial backing. Bringing together all my learning and best practices from the past 35 years – and not only that but being able to overlay a positive impact investment management process – certainly deepened this purpose. This, I have come to understand, is a very important human need, and it is extremely fulfilling to be able to offer a similar higher-order fulfilment to our clients, who are also motivated in this way.

I soon figured out the business would lend itself very well to digital search and, consequently, we could go to market with a sophisticated marketing plan, based on digital and social media. Fast forward three years, and I'm still astonished at how many wonderful people want to work with us with greater purpose towards their investments and their careers than they've ever enjoyed before.

Understanding my weaknesses in management capability, tech and digital channels, I sought the advice of two former clients to fill the void. Ashley Bell shared my vision from the get-go and became my co-founder and managing director. He is a formidable business leader and all-round übermensch. Elliot Muscant, with a stellar record in digital marketing, is similarly hyper-talented. As a valued adviser and investor, he has been critical in the positioning of the business and in our digital go-to-market strategy.

The Genesis of Path Financial

It's fulfilling to work in such a meaningful and purpose-driven environment where we're influencing consumers to make more ethical choices, and a wider market to make this type of investment more commonplace. It strikes me as being the obvious way forward because the markets *must* fix themselves, and we need to move to a more mindful money model.

We launched the business during the pandemic, which, while difficult in some ways, accelerated a transition to a more efficient and less carbon-intensive way of doing business. We had already set up paperless and virtual systems to be able to operate with fewer face-to-face meetings and less paper. I'm not sure the investing public was quite ready for this, but the pandemic necessitated change and we were incredibly well placed to move instantly to Zoom and other online platforms. This way of operating is now the norm for the whole financial planning industry, which is great when you consider the efficiency and the lower environmental footprint all round.

At the time of writing this book, I found the following statement on the Zoom website about the results during the pandemic:

> 'Zoom believes in caring for our environment. We estimate that by enabling millions of users to work from home during the COVID-19 pandemic, our platform helped our customers reduce their CO2 emissions by more than 55 million metric tons in 2020 – roughly equal to taking 11 million cars off the road.'

We wanted to recruit clients without having to burn hydrocarbons to travel to meet with them. I don't think the investing public was ready for video teleconferencing, but it was foisted upon them, and that played into our hands beautifully because in the early days of the business, we received enquiries from all over Britain, and as a broadly South-East-based company, we could now deal with them in a way we weren't able to before. It also meant we could recruit passionate advisers and administrative staff determined to make a difference regardless of their location. The best people are often the most committed to their values. Just as our client community was waiting for us to provide investment solutions, those seeking a higher purpose in their work were attracted to our organisation and found a home with us.

Investment up to this point in history has largely been around profit at any cost, but moving forward, for the sake of the planet, the priority must change to one of saving the planet at any cost. The moral imperative is more critical than profit, and for the market to persist at all, I believe it must correct itself. The system will inevitably have to adapt to survive, as human values and the urgency of the climate crisis unfold. And from a Maslovian hierarchy of needs perspective, the contribution we make to the most important things must become more important than selfishness and consumption. The rising consciousness of humans will shape behaviour so that we move away from investments and actions that have a negative impact towards solutions with a positive impact.

The Solution

Impact investment is the best solution out there to the climate crisis and to other inequalities we face. Two studies come to mind – one published several years ago by Nordea Bank showed that moving a lifetime's pension savings from traditional investment into impact investment had 27 times the impact of all other lifestyle changes to save carbon, and a more recent study by Make My Money Matter states 21 times. That's 21 times more impactful than stopping flying, going vegan, giving up your car, and all the other lifestyle changes. This data shows *how* you invest your money has a massive impact.

Opposite is an infographic which looks at some more impacts of moving just £100,000 from traditional "mindless" investment into positive impact investment. This is my own approximation and aggregation of data generally available in the public domain from a number of financial institutions. As we'll see later, data and measurement is very challenging in terms of accuracy. However, I believe that whilst only approximate, it does give an extremely compelling illustration of why it's important we start to wake up to the power and influence of our investments. And, more importantly, do something about it.

Currently, an investment in the FTSE 100 index is approximately two-thirds aligned with companies whose underlying products and services are negative or neutral from a people and planet perspective

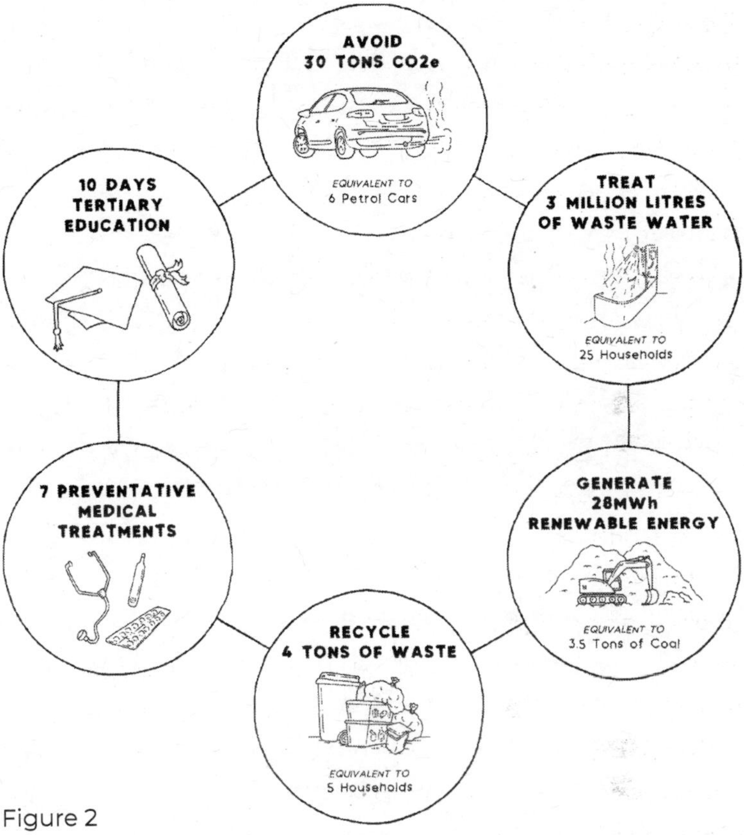

Figure 2

– and by far, the minority has any kind of social or environmentally positive impact – whereas a purposeful, positive impact fund will have something like 85% alignment with companies with products and services that are doing good from a people and planet perspective and contributing towards solutions (using the United Nations Sustainable Development Goals (SDGs) as a measure of alignment).

As David Attenborough said in his 2020 documentary *A Life on Our Planet*, 'It's crazy. Banks and pension funds are investing in fossil fuels, which jeopardises the very future people are saving for.'

What's astounding is that the financial advisory community doesn't seem to share this view. The latest data I've seen shows that 90% of financial advisers don't confront the question of investor preferences for impact investment. But when you ask consumers, 90% do want their investments to behave positively if they can. This means there's a vast gap between what the investing public wants and what the current model provides. This is currently being addressed by the UK financial regulator, the Financial Conduct Authority, with an ongoing consultation and new rules expected in terms of mandated client conversations as well as tighter regulation of measurement and definitions.

We must transform problems into opportunities – everyone can play a role in shifting us towards being more mindful about how we spend our money. We are the generation we've been waiting for. We are the generation our children and grandchildren need. We are the generation our planet and all earthlings need. Few of us will be around at the turn of the next millennium, but I believe we will all be judged. We're the ones with the power today, and it is in our hands to use that power and act accordingly. History will judge us heroes or villains. There's no reason for not turning money towards the more positive direction for people and the planet. It could be one of the most profound, meaningful and satisfying decisions we make in our lifetime.

CHAPTER 2

THE PROBLEM WITH PROFITS AT *ANY* PRICE

This book is one of optimism and hope. Its mission is to help promote and accelerate the uptake of positive impact investment and to inspire action by individuals and savers. This is the catalyst for the transformation needed.

This chapter will explore the problem of chasing profits without conscience. The beauty of a free-market model is that it's agile and efficient. Consumers will become more demanding and focus more on sustainability and the model will be forced to adapt and create a new paradigm. It needs to fix itself. It's by far the most dynamic force for change we have. The way to transform our economies is to have them generate solutions rather than problems, and this is the point of what's known as the impact investment model, which I will share with you.

Before we get to the solutions, we need to understand the problem and why the existing system can't fix it. We will look at what is wrong with the current model, issues it has created and the further problems that will emerge if it doesn't adapt.

The Existential Threat

That we face an existential threat is not now in any credible doubt. I don't intend to dwell on this, but it's clear we're already living unsustainably. We're in a position where we've had tremendous population growth over the last century. We've also enjoyed vastly improved living standards – certainly when measured by increased consumption – and this has put unprecedented pressure on the planet's resources. And the world's population has still not peaked. In simple terms, there is only so much planet to go around.

To put things into perspective, according to *Cowspiracy*, if you were to take the beef production of the United States and farm it organically, it would take up five times the land area of the United States, including all the lakes and deserts. So, we've already gone way beyond being able to live in a natural and organic way. Increases in consumption and population put ever more pressure on our natural resources. Fresh water is becoming a scarce resource and there are not enough easily usable rare earth elements. Phosphorous, an essential fertiliser ingredient to help feed our population, is predicted to run out this century.

New Year's Day 2023 was the hottest on record in

the UK. 2022 was the hottest year on record, with average temperatures exceeding 10°C for the first time since records began in 1884. Fifteen of the UK's warmest years on record have all occurred this century. Average temperatures are still steepling. Despite it being well rehearsed and familiar to all readers, it's worth reminding ourselves of the data.

Global Temperature Anomalies Compared to 20th Century Average

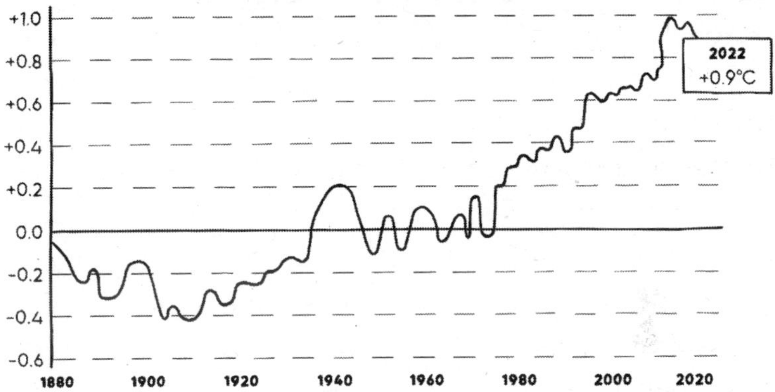

Figure 3

Just as obesity is now a bigger killer than famine, so are high temperatures becoming more threatening than extreme cold. As temperatures increase, so will the use of air conditioning. This, of course, consumes power, which, *if* it comes from fossil fuel, will exacerbate the warming with greater emissions. Yet another example of a feedback loop that will be created unless power generation moves completely to renewables.

The Current Business Model

We need a free-market model. That may be a contentious opinion, but there are undoubtedly efficiencies with it, and the fact remains that we are stuck with it anyway, certainly in the short and medium term. But the problem with the current way the market works is that it chases profit regardless of the consequences. Continuing as we are with an economic system that encourages linear and exploitative behaviours is not a viable option. We live in a world with finite resources. The only way the present model could successfully continue is to exploit more of our resources, which are simply not there. We need to move to a circular and sustainable model. And fast.

Certainly, since the post-World War Two era, corporates have focused on the way capital behaves and have maximised profit. And if that means exploiting people and the planet, then, as it stands, so be it. If companies want to exist for the long term, then they need to align their activities to ensure there will be a long term. The time for exploiting everything without a care is over.

It's no exaggeration to say that billions of people's lives depend on the success of what we might call a new "quiet revolution" to transform the capitalist model. Instead of being about profit at any cost, it's got to be about saving people's lives, and the planet, regardless of the cost. Adam Smith, author of *The Wealth of Nations*, published in 1776, and widely regarded as the father of modern economics, described how striving for profit results in everyone's best interests. I think this ethos needs to be updated so that everybody's best interest comes *before* striving for profit. It's a self-fulfilling logic tautology that if the planetary eco-system collapses, then less profit will be made. If everyone is dead, then no profit will be made. So actually it's probably fair to say markets will figure out that they need to adapt or die. Indeed, the impact investment movement may be the start of this transformation. But it needs a hefty shove to get the momentum going – and that's where more mindful money and you, dear reader, come in. To make it happen faster and stronger.

We have a responsibility to think about the way we invest our money and the purpose of the meaning it has, not only for us as individuals but for society. We must bring the impact of our investing to the heart of our society and place the outcomes at the heart of our economic system. We need to make financial decisions in a way that's consistent with achieving the highest impact for investors, while minimising the risk and threat to people and the planet.

There was a time when people thought about the impact of the negative consequences of investing only in terms of the financial risk, but now we must see investing as an opportunity, and review it through the lens of environmental, social and governance (ESG) factors. My philosophy is that we've got to disrupt current thinking to make sure there's a better profit by providing a supply to a greener alternative.

Innovative companies will profit as the laggards wither. This is the type of adaptation to consumer demands that can result in improving lives, reducing inequalities and saving the planet.

We have seen a big growth in the B Corp movement (Certified B Corporation). This is extremely important because it shows values being positioned at the heart of business decisions. I think it's now a given that most millennials and Gen Z consider it fundamental for businesses to espouse their values and walk their talk.

It's interesting speaking to Gen Z, whose parents were brought up in the post-Second World War era. For them, there was real austerity, suffering and shortage, and so when the economy improved, they felt they had the right to consume a lot. Success was measured by material wealth and status in terms of capital and goods, which is fascinating because that's not a human value. There's a backlash against that now, since we've realised that selfish over-consuming is not viable, sustainable or morally possible.

The Natural Hierarchy and Social Problems

While there's no denying standards of living in absolute terms have improved in recent decades, there has been an increasing polarisation of wealth amongst the middle classes. There's a saying I heard when I was a child, that "money goes to money", and in my experience, it's true. The more you have, the easier it is to make, and the less you have, the less opportunity you have. This means that the polarisation increases, and the "haves", as it were, have far too much, and the "have-nots" far too little.

This phenomenon is recognised in the most ancient of learned texts as true of human behaviour. In the Gospel of Matthew 13:12, we get the phrase "the Matthew effect". The outcome is relatively obvious: the wealthier I get, the more property I buy. Thus, I take housing stock out of the market, which creates scarcity and pushes prices up to the point of becoming affordable only to the better-off. Fewer people can afford to buy and they're forced to rent. This in turn raises rents and eventually trickles down to food prices. It has a circular and spiralling effect of inflating values over time.

Hierarchies are a natural, ancient phenomenon embedded in our common ancestry, stretching back over 300 million years, apparently to the earliest crustaceans. So, they're rather hard to avoid. We humans like social order and ranking – whether it's football leagues, levels of departmental responsibility, or competing for number of followers on social media, humans are happy to submit to some form of stratification. It's the natural way for us to organise ourselves.

The danger is in it becoming tyrannical. We are currently in an incredibly polarised situation, even more extreme than the 80/20 rule, or the Pareto Principle used to describe how 80% of consequences come from 20% of causes. (The principle was coined with reference to wealth, specifically the imbalance of land ownership in Italy.) As above, the notion is that the minority owns the majority. To some extent, we tolerate this, but I'm reminded of an Oxfam study in 2016 which claimed the wealthiest 1% were worth as much as the other 99% put together – a situation which anecdotally has been exacerbated through the COVID era, with the wealthiest billionaires becoming even wealthier. Many of these people are generous philanthropists; many are not. At the time of writing, we're going through what is being coined the "cost of living crisis". It would be better to reframe that slightly to the "inequality crisis". Sales of luxury brands are booming at the same time as rent and heating bills are causing others misery.

Although global living standards have improved dramatically, the difference between the relative wealth of the wealthy and the relative poverty of the poor has been stretched to a point where the system no longer seems fair. There is a real risk of rebellion and revolution, with the "tyranny" being overthrown and replaced with a new order. And, in due course, a new dominance hierarchy. This has been happening throughout history for millennia. Julius Caesar was reckoned to have a fortune, in today's terms, of $4.6 trillion – dwarfing the fortunes of modern-day billionaires. Beware the Ides of March ...

We ignore this risk of social disorder at our peril. It's not just the economic reality of wealth distribution but there being a mobilisation of the disenfranchised given the economic system no longer benefits them in any way at all. When homes become unaffordable or uninhabitable and resources scarce, people will be forced to flee.

We have a small window of opportunity to resolve this problem in a peaceful and measured way through the capital markets, and we had better get on with it or we're going to be in serious trouble.

Government

It seems unlikely we can look to governments to legislate for the necessary change. Indeed, the more neoliberal approach leaves markets undisturbed. Regrettably, politics is often influenced by short-term thinking linked to electoral cycles. It's a harsh truth for politicians – if they're being honest and realistic – that they need to tell us to reduce consumption, pay more taxes or curb our lifestyles, none of which is particularly a vote-winner. It's little wonder then that the can keeps getting kicked down the road, with an approach that advocates leaving the problem for the next lot while we pretend everything will be fine. This is akin to the ostrich wearing the emperor's new clothes – this method will not have optimal utility.

The Financial Industry

Al Gore, the former US vice president and Nobel Prize-winning environmentalist, said climate change is not just "your generation's life or death struggle" but the "biggest investment opportunity in history". According to an Invesco survey[1] in 2021, 85% of investors wanted their money to be invested sustainably.

So why is it that the transition to impact investment is so slow? One of the main issues is the financial industry being stuck in a rut of inertia, arrogance and ignorance. Based on my experience in the industry, I estimate 90% of advisers don't talk about these issues. This creates a hideous mismatch in terms of what people would like, compared with what the industry offers, in relation to the opportunity.

The financial world has a responsibility, not just to its shareholders, employees and suppliers but to the planet. Consumers will find their voice and will vote with their feet (or, more accurately, their purses and wallets). We are at the start of an inexorable march towards a pivot, where consumers will have a bigger role as stakeholders and influencers, and will only tolerate investment in firms showing higher and more authentic environmental and social standards. These companies will become more successful than those that are simply self-interested. Fund managers are increasingly turning their attention to better ESG scores since they have figured out that this maps to better financial performance. It's very sad so few financial advisers have translated this into what they offer their clients. As the gatekeepers to greener and more impactful funds, they have a bigger role to play, or they risk losing large numbers of clients.

---

1 https://www.investmentweek.co.uk/news/4033541/lack-knowledge-biggest-barrier-sustainable-investing-invesco

A Vicious Circle

Tragically, it's often the nations who've had the lightest touch on the planet that pay the heaviest price of global warming. When crops fail and livelihoods are threatened, vulnerability to exploitation and abuse increases. Marginalisation forces migration and leaves many with no alternative but to accept employment in extractive industries, such as industrialised agriculture, which involve deforestation. These sectors are associated with land concentration, pollution, soil erosion and excess water use, all of which, of course, contribute further to the very problem. This is an ironic and sad example of the type of vicious circle that can emerge from the problems we have covered here.

In future chapters, we'll look at how this can be transformed into a virtuous circle. With a little collective effort, the early adopters and innovators have brought us close to a more positive time, where there can be a far more satisfactory outcome for people and the planet. Inequalities are being addressed, and from an existential perspective, we can save ourselves with this approach.

The Danger of Procrastinating

There's an interesting TED Talk by Tim Urban about procrastination.[2] He makes the point that in delivering an outcome, we tend to leave things to the last minute. He tells the story of his dissertation, and how he was

2 https://www.youtube.com/watch?v=arj7oStGLkU

driven by the deadline. We might have six months to deliver something, but so many of us will leave it right to the last minute to take the required action. Tim talks about the "monkey brain", which puts things off because it just wants to have fun. He goes on to say that the thing that saves the day is the panic monster, who turns up immediately before the deadline so we get the necessary task done at the last possible minute.

The problem with relying on this procrastinator's model is that it depends on there being a deadline to panic about. Rather like the climate crisis, with no hard deadline the panic monster won't show up until it's too late. We've got to employ the grown-up brain to run the show rather than let the monkey brain be in charge and delay the necessary action. It's a bit like watching your parents grow old – you don't notice the changes when they're gradual. It's the same with the changing climate. It's happening so slowly that we don't see the effects every day. Most of us are in denial because that's easier than facing the reality that we're living unsustainably and we still equate materialism with success. There's little appreciation for the planet's resources, which are finite. 'There's no plan B because there's no planet B' comes to mind.

We must position our investments accordingly because increased consumption is not the future for people and the planet. Or profit. There is a small group of people who own more wealth than everybody else on the planet combined, and I don't think we should rely on their philanthropy to solve climate and societal issues. The wealthiest people in society can usually find ways to pay the lowest percentages of tax, so we have this inequality where the wealthier you are, the less you contribute to the fiscal system, which then has to rely on philanthropy. Fortunately, there are many good-hearted capitalists with very generous legacies, such as the Bill & Melinda Gates Foundation. The capitalist model needs to adapt to constrain profit to be more redistributive, stop exploitation of workers and invest in people and the planet.

We're overleveraged on debt, and debt enables us to have a growth beyond our means. We're living too far from work, so multiple car ownership for families is a cultural norm, and because there's no smoking gun right now, it's hard for people to see there's a problem. There may be a few days of extremely high temperatures, but then we go back to living as if everything is okay again. It's all happening at a glacial pace, you might say, but the glaciers are melting. We criticise China for having a massive environmental footprint without realising we've exported our problem to them. Rather than taking responsibility for the things we consume, we outsource it to far-away countries, who then ship our goods across the ocean after manufacturing them, and create the carbon footprint.

Future Problems

Continuing as we are will lead to more marginalised parts of the earth, scarcity of resources and social breakdown. Under the duress that would ensue, civilised behaviour and global co-operation would deteriorate. It really doesn't have to be that way – there are adequate resources to go around. The system needs to be re-organised, and we must move to a more circular economy. Impact investment encourages all of this, which is why I'm so passionate about it.

CHAPTER 3

WHY GREEN MONEY IS THE ANSWER

Chapter 2 examined problems we're facing – the challenges and the headwinds – in terms of the impact the Anthropocene Epoch (the most recent period of our history) is having on people and the planet. However well meaning governments are (and, let's face it, many are not), they're just not equipped to innovate. And philanthropy and charity will only go so far.

Capitalism and our free-market approach, as it currently stands, is an efficient mechanism for achieving profit, regardless of the cost. As such, the consequence of possible "bad behaviour" is part of the problem. Progress is inhibited by outdated perceptions of what it takes to make a financial return and by closed-minded old-fashioned ideas which financial intermediaries and, to a lesser extent, fund managers hold onto. But for progress to become the solution, it just needs a decent nudge in the right direction and to gather momentum. I believe this nudge can come from the investing public.

Mother Nature, or the natural world, has the habit of fixing itself whenever there's a problem, doing all it can to get back into equilibrium. I think that's where we are with money now, and that if we're to have a future at all, it's time for the capitalist model to fix itself.

I'm reminded of the old quote attributed to Einstein, that the definition of insanity is continuing to do the same thing and expecting a different result. Clearly, if we want a different result, we've got to change what we're doing. Impact investment, mindful money or caring capitalism – call it what you will – is about changing our investment behaviour. We must stop thinking of investment only in terms of associated risks, and consider creating a better future and making a positive impact on the planet and its population.

The Spectrum

There's a traditional view that there is a spectrum of capital. Capitalism, red in tooth and claw, is at one end of the spectrum. It puts profit ahead of all other considerations with a win-lose mentality, where for me to win, you must lose. We might call it the "lunch is for wimps" approach from the film *Wall Street*, or the selfishness and hedonism portrayed in *The Wolf of Wall Street*.

At the other, far, end of the spectrum, and the antithesis of that approach, sits philanthropy, or charitable giving. This is where you don't expect the return *of* your money, let alone a return *on* your money. The ultimate impact on this spectrum is created by giving your money away. Logically, when presented like this, it might seem that the minute you move away from *The Wolf of Wall Street* approach towards the philanthropy end of the spectrum, investment returns should diminish, which, if you're a red in tooth and claw capitalist, could be a problem.

The great news is we don't need to do all or nothing, because that old spectrum doesn't accurately reflect the situation. The question of impact on investment, or doing well by doing good, doesn't sit on that linear spectrum and is in a completely new space.

The Win-Win Solution

Impact investment offers a win-win solution that aligns money with positive outcomes for the planet. The world of financial services is changing fast. People want excellent investments, as they always have, but today they want their investments to do good things. This means we're moving away from a position where a pure financial return is the only consideration, and social and climate change issues will now be viewed in terms of opportunity.

We're heading from the pure profit model to a place where the mindful investor wants to invest with a conscience but doesn't want to compromise on financial return – where successful solutions for people and the planet will provide healthy investment returns. The Global Impact Investing Network (GIIN) would say we're at the dawn of impact investment. I believe this approach needs to be at the heart of society and at the heart of the economic system, because it offers positive returns, positive impact, and minimises risk.

Let's look at one of the game changers. Elon Musk, CEO of Tesla Motors, has single-handedly progressed the electric vehicle (EV) market. This is a classic example where one person's vision has tipped a market significantly early and had such a massive impact that it's now the only way things are going. It's a complete shift from "infernal" combustion engines. The ultimate technology remains to be seen, but petrol and diesel engines are becoming a thing of the past. The death warrant has already been signed. We're beyond the watershed and this reality has manifested. Early adopters of Musk's EV strategy have done extremely well financially. We've now got a situation where the government is being criticised for not having adequate infrastructure to support the number of EVs people are buying. It's a classic example of governments failing to lead and typically being left trying to catch up with the private sector once change has been instigated.

Using the transportation analogy, let's consider where we are in the evolution of the economic cycle. I often reflect on the turn of the 19th century, when the transportation technology of the day was the stagecoach. Then came the advent of the train. If stagecoach companies thought they were in the stagecoach business, they would have just tried to build better stagecoaches. But if they'd realised they were in the transportation business, they would have adopted the new technology – the train. Those that moved with the technology developments survived, and those that didn't went bankrupt.

> *'If I had asked people what they wanted, they would have said a faster horse'* – Henry Ford.

One risk for investors today is investing in companies that don't know what business they're in. The obvious example is those that think they're oil companies. Their model is extracting hydrocarbons and burning them. A large amount of their value is predicated on identified reserves that are still in the ground. The balance sheet value is potentially huge – but only if they get the oil out and sell it. There are headwinds against this happening. The price of renewables continues to plummet, which is a major competitive factor. We, as a society of consumers, will at some point (hopefully sooner rather than later) disallow them to continue to dig up oil and burn it. That means the balance sheet value will no longer be accurate. We call this phenomenon "stranded assets", and it may well catch unwary investors out. Unless, of course, these companies understand they're energy companies, or even infrastructure companies, and adapt to where they need to be positioned. From an investment perspective, the way forward is for companies to stop trying to frustrate progress, which will get them into trouble with their investors, and put money into progressive companies that are contributing to solutions.

Capitalism is a Motivating Force

Capitalism is an immense and motivating force. It just needs some encouragement to stop putting profit as the only goal, and to have better outcomes as the motivation. We know it's a sensible investment decision. We know it's a pragmatic approach for the planet. Maslow's Hierarchy of Needs says that once we satisfy our basic needs, we move into a higher level of what matters. To create this impact with our investments, our thinking needs to change. I think we are starting to see the emergence of an evolution or revolution where companies also get to a point where their basic needs are met and they move to a higher level of showing social and environmental integrity.

We're talking about a massive social environmental challenge, but we've got a multi-trillion-pound force behind us which can instigate sweeping changes. Change must come from the mindset and behaviour of investors, philanthropists, entrepreneurs, social organisations and big business, and from the public getting a chance to vote for positive impact at the centre of decision-making. To avert disaster, we can't carry on with a system that doesn't actively seek to make a positive impact and continues to create negative consequences.

Humankind has made huge strides in an incredibly short time. We have the capacity to change and find the answer. The distribution of opportunity and outcome can be fairer, and it is a necessary imperative. Maslow tells us that this is possible – but investment principles also mean that more social factors have to be considered because the best investments will have the best ESG scores.

Our economies will evolve to generate solutions rather than problems. Billions of people's lives depend on the success of this impact revolution. It's a question of taking personal responsibility and choosing to live with purpose.

The Impact Revolution

We have seen phenomenal progress in the first 20 years of this century, in what we might call the Tech Revolution. The next 20 years have to see similar transformational change for the environment, in what will be the Impact Revolution.

Millennials and Gen Z are typically more conscious of where their money goes. In my experience, there are also many older people who are increasingly mindful of this impact revolution – thinking about their grandchildren's lives, and the planet they might inhabit. Ahead of the next century, which is a very long timeline, those who will be impacted and those whose loved ones will be impacted are making this transition already. I see a pincer movement happening which will also draw in the middle-aged.

People will no longer tolerate what I call "mindless" investments, or those lacking a social conscience. As we discussed in the previous chapter, research shows that 90% of people surveyed want their investments to have a sustainability dimension. The problem is, the financial service industry isn't delivering, because so many financial advisers aren't knowledgeable or confident to advise on impact investment. There's a massive gulf between what's demanded by the public when they're given the opportunity to consider what they want, and the opportunities and options on offer.

Simon Sinek, in his seminal TED Talk 'Start With Why', explains how consumers are increasingly getting behind company ethos and are basing their consumer choices on the positioning, attitudes and value of the companies they buy from. This is exemplified by the clothing company Patagonia and many other B Corps (including Path Financial!).

According to a consumer culture report,[3] 71% of consumers prefer buying from companies aligned with their values, and 83% of millennials say buying from companies that share their values is important.

'Companies that fail to adapt to climate change will go bankrupt,' predicted Mark Carney, the governor of the Bank of England, in 2019. He also said that capitalism is part of the solution and great fortunes will be made along the way, with which I

3 https://www.5wpr.com/new/research/consumer-culture-report/

wholeheartedly agree. Humans are above all goal-oriented problem-solvers.

Al Gore defines sustainable investing as "improving quality of life without borrowing from the future", and that "it has the magnitude of the Industrial Revolution but the speed of the Digital Revolution".

Larry Fink, the chair and chief executive officer of BlackRock, in 2020 said, 'I believe we are on the edge of a fundamental reshaping of finance.'

This is the age where finance is now being defined by the cost to the environment and the climate. Businesses have a responsibility to shareholders, employees and suppliers – and the world as a whole. Finance is transforming, and I believe there's never been a better opportunity to put our pensions to work, not only to fund our old age **but to make sure we have a future**.

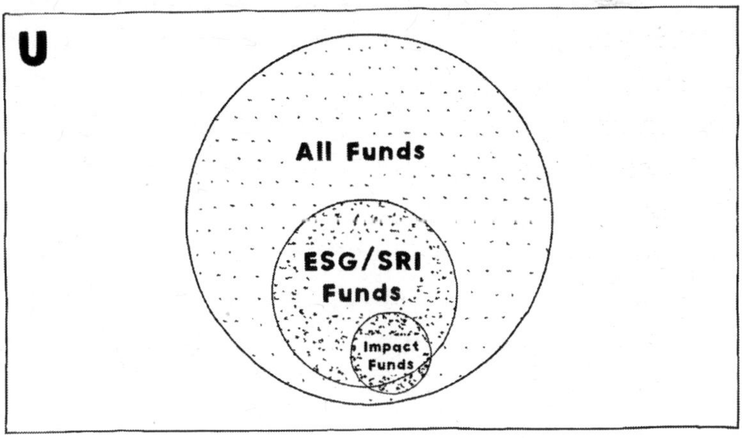

Figure 4: The Investment Universe

As you can see in the Venn diagram of investment, U is the universal set of all you could choose to invest in, and when it comes to pensions and other liquid, long-term investments, most people invest in funds. The fund universe in the UK comprises something like 8,000 funds, and the majority are run for optimal profit. Of these funds, a fraction claim to do some screening out of investments which are not deemed ethical. That's about as far as the industry has advanced – not investing in things which are viewed unethical, based on subjective definitions.

The solution is to go far beyond that and rather than just screening out the negative, screening in the positive. There's a small subset of ethical funds which operate in this way. These funds comprise only companies whose products and services provide solutions for the good of people and the planet.

The Evolution of Ethical and Impact Investment (an Alphabet Soup of Jargon)

Let's look at the history and evolution of "ethical" investment, and the main jargon, so you are familiar with the terminology. The earliest origins of ethical investment can be traced back to faith groups. The Quakers in the 18th century prohibited members from participating in the slave trade. John Wesley, a founder of Methodism, wrote a paper on socially responsible investing (SRI).

The modern era matured somewhat from the 1960s through to the 1980s but was still very much focused on avoiding the so-called sin stocks – alcohol, tobacco, arms and pornography. Islamic investment principles are similarly aligned. According to Sharia rules, compliance with Islamic finance principles leads to a more ethical and just society. The idea is that it achieves balance between religion, family, life, intellect and property.

Until recently, this was as far as ethical investment had progressed. It was perceived as a backwater for people with strong religious views, and as a crackpot approach to accepting inferior investment returns through putting their principles first. This was hardly the prevailing attitude of the latter quarter of the 20th century, which was exemplified by Thatcherism, Reaganomics and a "greed is good" materialism.

The old faith-based definitions took little or no account of environmental factors. There was nothing wrong with coal and oil investment from a faith-based perspective. But, with climate change emerging into our consciousness and us having well-documented evidence for the causes of environmental degradation and climate change, the old definitions are no longer fit for purpose. There has also been increasing attention paid to the social impacts of businesses and what constitutes decent or abusive business practices. In recent years, we have seen the emergence of three key measurement metrics relating to companies' ESG behaviours and impacts. The more contemporary term is ESG investing. This also encompasses the concept of divestment, which we might define as being the deliberate selling of stocks in a portfolio on ethical grounds, with a view to "punishing" companies guilty of abuses.

A more up-to-date list of ethical exclusions today would include:

- Alcohol and tobacco manufacture and sale
- Armaments, controversial weapons and military contracts
- Poor environmental practice
- Palm oil and deforestation
- Coal, mining, oil and gas
- Poor labour standards
- Gambling
- Air freight
- Unhealthy food
- Animal agriculture.

There is no universally agreed definition of "ethical", so the above list is somewhat of a pick-and-mix and may vary according to individual moral standpoint. The different terms can be confusing. The simple answer is to concentrate on investments which do positive things for people and the planet by investing in:

- Education for all
- Healthcare and social care
- Financial inclusion and insurance
- Sustainable water and safe sanitation
- Clean and renewable energy
- Sustainable transport and infrastructure

- Recycling and circular economy
- Protecting natural resources
- Sustainable and healthy food
- Diversity
- New climate technology solutions.

Let's talk about what a positive investment might be. The United Nations (UN) has published their sustainable development goals, a set of 17 strategic things they believe need to be addressed to make the world a fairer and more sustainable place. They describe it as:

> The 2030 Agenda for Sustainable Development, adopted by all United Nations Member States in 2015, provides a shared blueprint for peace and prosperity for people and the planet, now and into the future.[4] At its heart are the 17 Sustainable Development Goals (SDGs), which are an urgent call for action by all countries – developed and developing – in a global partnership. They recognize that ending poverty and other deprivations must go hand-in-hand with strategies that improve health and education, reduce inequality, and spur economic growth – all while tackling climate change and working to preserve our oceans and forests.

Companies, products and services that exploit people and the planet are at variance with this. Other companies, products and services are very much

4 https://sdgs.un.org/2030agenda

aligned with the solutions we seek, to achieve a fairer and more sustainable world. These minor changes need to be made, to tilt capitalism onto the path of a more conscious capitalism and mindful money approach, which means people giving more thought to the choices they make about their investments.

The SDGs are in danger of being missed if they do not get an urgent and sizeable increase in funding. Although sustainability has become a major talking point in the past few years, especially as the world looks to build back greener after COVID-19, a lack of both public and private investment is hampering progress.

According to the UN, an estimated $5–7 trillion a year is needed to realise the 2030 Agenda for Sustainable Development worldwide.[5] The international community has made clear that the private sector plays, and will play, a fundamental role in the realisation of this agenda, and in the delivery of the sustainable development goals in the years to come.

The Rockefeller Foundation[6] asserts that "the key to financing and achieving the SDGs lies in mobilizing a greater share of the $200+ trillion in private capital investment flows toward development efforts ...". Large-scale funders participating in a Rockefeller Foundation-hosted design thinking

---

5 https://www.unglobalcompact.org/take-action/action/globalallianceforsdgfinance

6 https://en.wikipedia.org/wiki/Rockefeller_Foundation

workshop concluded that "while there is a moral imperative to achieve the SDGs, failure is inevitable if there aren't drastic changes to how we go about financing large-scale change".

Unless we point people in the right direction, how would it occur to them to change something they don't understand? It's perfectly reasonable not to beat ourselves up for past choices, but when given exposure to better options, then why not make that positive choice? This is why I am writing this book, and what I would like to help you do.

CHAPTER 4

IMPACT INVESTMENT IN ACTION

We've explored how impact investment is a strategy which targets companies or industries that produce social-environmental benefits. Impact investors often seek to support renewable energy, electric cars, microfinance, sustainable agriculture, property, and social initiatives which they believe to be worthwhile.

This chapter will offer some practical examples of impact investment in action, i.e. types of investments made with the intention of generating positive measurable impact alongside a healthy financial return.

Chapter 3 looked at the capital spectrum, with the capitalist model at one end and philanthropy at the other. My contention is that impact investment transcends this spectrum with higher returns and all-round better outcomes.

With this new way of thinking, we're moving away

from dinosaur companies with destructive products and services that will end up as stranded assets – like oil having to remain in the ground. Investing in dinosaur companies no longer makes financial sense, whereas aligning with innovative companies that create solutions and technological advances can achieve superior investment returns.

The ABC of Impact Investment

I simply call the process of impact investment the "ABC":

A – Avoid harm
B – Benefit stakeholders
C – Contribute to solutions

In every facet of investment – from property through to cash, bonds, equities and alternatives like microfinance – there are opportunities to have a more sustainable, and possibly even superior, investment alternative than the traditional options.

Five Key Areas for Diversifying a Green Investment Portfolio

We will focus on a sensible structure for model investment portfolios in a later chapter. Broadly, though, most investment portfolios comprise a combination of the following assets:

- Cash
- Bonds
- Property
- Equities (shares)
- Microfinance and other alternatives

We can achieve the same degree of diversification as a traditional investment model, using a green, sustainable, more impactful alternative, without diminishing the financial performance of the portfolio.

Your Pension Has an Impact

The big question is, how do we give capitalism the helping hand it needs to achieve a redefinition of its purpose? Consumer choice is the answer. When we think of pensions or investments, the two words that usually come to mind are "complex" and "boring". With pensions, in particular, I've noticed people's eyes quickly glaze over. It's like a black box into which stuff disappears, and engagement is extremely low.

What I aim to do is drag that complex and boring topic to a simplified and interesting place. As consumers, we've got an idea of some things we think we should be doing to support the environment. Some of the "shoulds" might involve flying less frequently, buying an electric vehicle, cutting down or cutting out our meat and dairy consumption, drinking oat milk rather than almond milk, or not eating avocados because they've got a high carbon footprint. The list goes on ...

What we don't immediately think of is the impact our money has, but every time we put money into this boring and complex black box, where we don't think about it, the money still has some type of impact, whether good or bad, or somewhere in between. If we ignore this sobering fact, then we unconsciously abdicate our responsibility for the behaviour of our money. If we're mindful, then we can choose to put our money in more positive investments.

Impact Investment Examples and Solutions

Cash

Investing in cash is usually done by depositing with a bank in return for a rate of interest. The interest banks pay depositors is generated by lending the same money to borrowing customers. Regrettably, the Banking on Climate Change[7] report confirms that the world's largest banks are continuing to finance fossil fuel exploration and production. Lending is still flowing to arctic oil, tar sands, deep-sea oil and gas exploration, which all have hugely damaging environmental consequences. Most UK high street banks are involved in lending to companies that have unsustainable activities, and so there is a strong case for not investing cash with these banks.

The better alternative is to deposit cash with banks that support a more sustainable and inclusive agenda, but unfortunately there are very few. Triodos is one such positive impact bank, with well-defined boundaries around what it will and won't do. Although small, sustainability and positive change are at the heart of its operations. This includes deposits and

7 https://www.bankingonclimatechaos.org/bankingonclimatechange2020/

investment ISAs (Individual Savings Accounts) right through to crowdfunding.

Bonds

First, let's think about what a bond is. A bond is a loan, at a fixed rate of interest for a fixed period. Typically issued in one-hundred-pound units, the loan is repayable at the end of the loan period. This gives the investor certainty about the rate of interest they'll get and about getting their money back (as long as the issuing body is still solvent). This is why bonds are called "fixed-interest securities". Bonds are considered relatively safe investments. Government bonds issued by very financially strong countries, such as Germany, are considered amongst the safest and will pay the lowest rate of interest. At the other end of the spectrum lies debt issued by financially shaky companies, which get the moniker "junk bonds" since they have a high chance of default (where the investor loses their money but is paid an extremely high rate of interest). In between, there are a number of bonds that offer a more attractive rate of interest than banks and with an acceptable level of risk. Bonds are often traded and prices can fluctuate. Values of bonds can also go down if interest rates rise sharply or unexpectedly – which we saw in 2022. Similarly, if economic sentiment is very negative, then the fear of default rises and bonds trade at below "par".

Government Bonds

Government bonds (also known as gilts or gilt-edged securities in the UK and some Commonwealth countries) are sovereign debts. Bonds issued by governments are considered very secure because governments seldom default on their debt, therefore the interest payments and the capital redemption are stable. Regular government debt is seldom "green", though, since what governments tend to spend money on is not in line with positive impact or ethical principles – weapons, invasions, subsidies for animal agriculture, oil.

In late 2022, a new coal mine was sanctioned in the UK. (Yes, the one that wasn't given the go-ahead in 2021, which would have looked bad when the country was hosting COP26.)

Recently, though, we have seen both "green gilts" and "green savings bonds" issued by the UK National Savings & Investments (NS&I). By the end of 2021, £16 billion was raised by the UK government from green gilts issuance for projects like zero-emissions buses, offshore wind, and schemes to decarbonise homes and buildings. The order book was 12 times oversubscribed, which shows the enormous demand for the UK's green gilts. The combined size of the two transactions now means the UK is one of the top three biggest national issuers of green bonds in the world. By issuing green gilts at several maturity points, the UK has set a baseline for green sterling debt, making it easier for companies to price their own green bonds.

Green gilts have also demonstrated the benefits of green finance to business, with high demand for green products leading to better rates for issuers.

Corporate Bonds

Corporate bonds are very similar in concept to government bonds; typically, financial markets might lend money to a large company that pays a fixed rate of interest, for example 5% over ten years. The loan then gets repaid at the end of the period. These have generally been considered safe investments, because the markets are lending to a large corporate, there's a fixed rate of interest and, as long as the company doesn't go bust, they'll be repaid after the fixed period. This may work financially, but it isn't helping the planet. Also, it's riskier than government bonds since the possibility of default from a corporate is higher than from a government – and there is a risk spectrum to consider, given financially weaker companies represent much more of a risk than financially secure ones. Corporate bonds are generally investible for companies that align with an investor's ethical principles, but many will not.

Green Bonds

A green bond is another type of corporate bond. In this instance, the money is raised by an organisation for a specific sustainable project. It's one of those unusual areas where companies that might be screened out due to negative ESG factors become investible. Take, for example, a fossil fuel company that's trying to fund a shift to more renewable products and services, with a view to moving into the sustainable arena. Green bonds can be made available to them when the project in question is demonstrably within the ethical and impact criteria. We might think of it as a kind of "rehab" finance to encourage and facilitate transition and speed up change.

Making Meaningful Social Impact with Bond Investments

Bonds are typically IOUs issued by governments and corporates. But with impact investment, it could be debt issued by a charity. One example to highlight is the EdenTree Responsible and Sustainable Short Dated Bond Fund. One borrower in this fund is Golden Lane Housing, a London charity and investment bond which makes a tangible, meaningful difference to people's lives. The charity's purpose is to create or provide housing for people with learning difficulties or other challenges to allow them to live a more independent lifestyle or to live safely.

Investment into a fund such as this directly increases the availability of accommodation to people who desperately need it and probably can't otherwise find it. Without investors, the money would not be there. In this example, the risk of default is tiny because local government guarantees or pays the rent and the fund owns the property, which is a tangible asset. Beyond that, the fund manager has a charitable focus – all the profit is donated to charity.

It's the ultimate "virtuous circle", where money's taken out of potentially damaging industries and invested in a way which makes an improvement to people's lives. The profit is then recycled back into the charitable economy. At the bond end of the spectrum, this is an example of where impact investment clearly creates a demonstrable difference, as opposed to just being lost in the financial system.

Property

Property investment can also be impactful. It's likely there'll be legislative changes to make buildings more efficient in terms of energy consumption. And there is a limited supply of the types of buildings that can be retrofitted, or adapted. So, investors who are quick to identify suitable buildings that can be upgraded with energy-saving options will be rewarded with bigger investment returns.

As energy efficiency standards are required to become more rigorous, this will involve things like:

- insulation of walls and roofs
- fitting of solar panels
- more energy-efficient glass to retain heat in the winter and reflect heat in the summer
- more energy-efficient air conditioning and heating systems – air source and ground source, and heat exchanges to create lower carbon buildings.

The buildings that can't be converted to meet the emerging standards will naturally be less desirable, possibly even uninhabitable depending on how rigorous legislation becomes. This presents an opportunity for investors. Two buildings might look similar, but if one can be retrofitted to be energy efficient and the other can't, then the one that can be converted ultimately will be the more valuable asset and attract a higher rental income or sale price.

Equities

Investment in stocks and shares – or equities, as I will term them – is not well understood. People don't seem to understand equity investment in the way they understand property investment.

With property, you buy a unit and hope it goes up in value. In the meantime, the rent generated pays you an income. Simple. It's really the same with shares. You buy shares in a company and hope they will go up. And the company pays you "rent" for owning the shares by way of a dividend – a percentage of the profits. If you buy well, for example in a company that is growing rapidly, then the dividend will increase every year, the profits will increase every year and the share price will keep going up. Shares are a dynamic way of keeping pace with inflation and attaching your investment to the "real" economy of companies that operate in the world.

We saw earlier how there can be challenges with investing in dinosaur companies, with the risk of stranded assets. On the flip side, there are opportunities to invest in companies that are well positioned to take advantage of what the world and its people need.

There's any number of possible areas where emerging investments offer an interesting opportunity. There will be winners and losers and some will overleverage and go bust, and others will storm ahead to huge success. We should always be cautious about citing particular examples and becoming hostage to fortune but some may be useful. Whatever their future financial outcomes may be, they have rewarded early investment.

This reminds me: if there are two arts to stock investment, once you have identified a share to buy, they are (1) when to buy and (2) when to sell. Many people buy too late due to fear – they want to see the stock go up before they commit to buying. Then, they're too late to sell due to greed – they've seen the shares going up and assume they'll keep going up, with anti-gravity magic, and hang on for too long. One of my personal tactics, which has worked many times, is once a share has doubled in value, sell half. Then you have your original investment back to redeploy elsewhere and whatever the share does after that stands you in nothing.

Anyway, here are two examples where big returns could have been had and also where a timely and strategic exit would have been sensible. (One of the advantages of using professional investment and fund managers is that these timing decisions are delegated to them and there is less likelihood of emotional decision-making – the scourge of the amateur investor.)

Renewable Energy

Renewable energy is an obvious choice for impact investments, so I want to mention Ørsted, which was formerly called Danish Oil and Natural Gas (DONG). They were in the oil and natural gas business until about ten years ago, but they made a strategic decision to become a renewable energy company. At the time of writing, they have transitioned to 95% renewable energy and they're currently the largest wind farm operator in the world. The financial performance of that company, for those that had the vision to invest early, has been tremendous as they've been ahead of the curve of developing offshore wind farms. This is an example of a company which has performed better than oil companies over the last decade but made a significant transition to clean energy and will not be in a position of holding stranded assets.

Boris Johnson said in his time as prime minister he wanted the North Sea to become the "Saudi Arabia of wind". The North Sea is home to the world's largest offshore wind farm and, according to a report, Ørsted[8] has installed much of the UK's offshore wind capacity. It's fascinating that an area traditionally famous for its oil could become an area where renewable energy

8 https://www.bbc.co.uk/news/av/science-environment-57519392

thrives in the same way as solar energy in the desert in the Middle East.

From the point of view of the investor, investing in renewables is a win-win because they won't have a "dirty investment" on their hands, which they would if they were investing in a fossil fuel company. But there is an even bigger impact when trying to influence fossil fuel companies to do what Ørsted has already done. Once the polluting companies realise what the damage of being shunned as an investment will do to their share price, they'll make the change towards more renewable energy.

There's an enormous opportunity in "catching the wave" and encouraging companies to make that transition. Tidal energy, anyone?

A Revolution in Recycling

There are some surprising examples of companies moving towards more sustainable options, one of which reminds me of when I was a kid. In those days, if you bought a glass bottle of lemonade, you got a few pence back for returning it to the shop. Anyone over the age of 50 who lived in Britain as a child will probably remember this scheme fondly. My mates and I used to go around the bins of the east end of Edinburgh, collecting discarded bottles, to return to the shop. That's how we supplemented our pocket money – it was my earliest entrepreneurial foray. I would love to see this scheme revived as it's a wonderful example of going back to basics and rewarding enterprising individuals for making a big difference to the planet.

A company called Tomra does a similar thing while harnessing the latest technology. It uses a reverse vending machine idea, where you feed plastic bottles into their machines and receive a credit. It's known as a "revolution in recycling", and seems an effective way of recycling plastic, while rewarding people's efforts.

We're seeing these early opportunities emerging in the circular economy, in production, which involves things like sharing, leasing, refurbishing and recycling. Unilever, which is increasingly re-using plastic to recycle, rather than making new plastic bottles, and even a long-established company like Pepsi are transitioning towards this model.

Second-hand clothes are super-trendy now. And brands such as Patagonia and Finisterre are deliberately making apparel to last, and which can be repaired, in contrast to disposable fast fashion. Globally, we consume 80 billion pieces of clothing every year. According to Patrick Grant from *The Great British Sewing Bee*, there are already enough garments in existence to clothe the next six generations of people on the planet. The dyeing of fast-fashion textiles alone contributes 3% of carbon emissions – about 50% more than aviation! Investment in "slow fashion" seems like it could be a good idea.

Microfinance

We would typically include microfinance in a positive impact portfolio. Historically, we know that women and girls have been marginalised in finance, and, in many countries, men still control the money. This is the reality for many women who don't have the opportunity to be empowered around money. Microfinance can be particularly helpful for women in these situations.

Let's say someone is working in a global south country, making a given product, and they have an extremely limited budget, or they're beholden to a lender for their supplies. If they must borrow money to get their raw materials and are not credit worthy of a reputable lender, they might borrow from a local moneylender who charges extortionate rates of interest. How can they break free of the cycle where most of their profits end up in the money lender's pocket? This is where microfinance can provide a small loan – even a hundred dollars can be enough to enable someone to buy their raw materials at a reasonable rate of interest that they can repay to a reputable provider. It works because the textile maker's motivation to repay the loan is extremely high, knowing they can borrow again. This allows them access to bigger loans and to harness more of the profit to reinvest in business expansion, which gives them the opportunity to create financial freedom rather than financial exploitation.

There are many success stories where people have been able to use microfinance to lift themselves out of poverty and pay for their children's education. They've also provided employment for their community, which creates financial inclusion for people who ordinarily wouldn't have access to a fair financial system.

Microfinance Success Story

Rwandan entrepreneur Jacqueline Mukacyemayire became a phenomenal microfinance success story through her thriving business. The first loan she received was for $100, which she shared between eight women to start a small sewing business, making dresses with a borrowed machine. Jacqueline was a seamstress trapped in a vicious cycle. Thanks to the reasonable rate of interest, she accumulated enough profit to qualify for a second loan of $200, when she then bought her first sewing machine.

By 2015, Jacqueline employed 15 full-time staff and had received six microloans from VisionFund, the microfinance subsidiary of World Vision. She was able to create a profitable business and afford to send her four children, including an orphan the family adopted, to school and her daughter to college. Her next dream was to set up a factory to make fabric, instead of importing it, and to employ 12 people.

Microfinance can deliver a win-win combination of high levels of impact together with reliable rates of return. There are good financial returns for people who provide microfinance as well, so it's another win-win.

Micro-Cap Investment

The government offers tax relief incentives to enterprise initiative schemes (EIS) and venture capital trusts (VCTs) where they are seed-type investments in extremely small companies. Unlike for listed or more mainstream equities, which most people invest in, HMRC offers a 30% tax relief for those with a higher risk tolerance. This means the investor effectively only pays 70 pence in the pound for investments into more speculative, but highly impactful, ventures. For emerging technologies and high-risk investment in small companies, there are opportunities to get involved at the higher end of the risk spectrum. Many of these businesses are in high-impact areas. EIS and VCT schemes encourage this type of entrepreneurialism, while giving investors some baked-in downside protection.

There's a lot more money being made available via the impact model now, through backing diverse entrepreneurs and social movements. Black Lives Matter and #MeToo resounded well beyond the 2020 protests on the streets and have spurred investors to act on systemic, racial and gender inequalities, especially when it comes to backing talent. Historically, there's been less money for diversity and inclusion, but it's something we're seeing the impact investment movement turning towards.

Delivering Through Diversity, a McKinsey &

Company report, concludes that companies in the top quarter of gender diversity were 25% more likely to have above average profitability than companies in the lowest quarter. And that boost was even more apparent for firms demonstrating the same top-tier levels of ethnic diversity, with 36% more likely to have above average profitability. This research validates how those investors who ignore this sea change not only risk missing the opportunity to get more capital to diverse communities, but also positioning their portfolio to make better returns.

I believe there's nothing that can't be achieved in this higher-impact model. And we're only just getting started, so the opportunities are exciting and rewarding.

CHAPTER 5

MEASURING IMPACT

All investments have an impact since all the companies we invest in have activities which create an impact. My aim is to enlighten you about the fundamentals of impact investment measurement, which is in its infancy. I won't bore you with technicalities but will share the basics so you know what to look out for when you evaluate your potential investments.

> *'If you can't measure it, you can't manage it'*
>
> – Peter Drucker

This famous maxim is as relevant to this topic as it is to many others. One difficulty of this type of investment is that the measurements we use (E, S & G) are not like binary measures. They are subjective on a linear scale. We can attempt to measure impact with the help of the following:

Environmental impact (E) relates to pollution, which covers things like water management, greenhouse gas emissions and renewable energy waste.

Social impact (S) relates to things such as labour standards, workforce productivity, supply chain practices and talent management.

Governance (G) is board diversity, accountability, bribery, corruption, lobbying activity, etc.

These are the non-financial aspects of a company's performance, but they are still key contributors to its bottom line. In the past, the investment industry tended to measure only the financial performance of a company or fund – things like turnover, profitability, profit margins, the growth in the share price, the growth in the dividends and many technical measures related to financial performance: alpha, beta, Sharpe ratio, standard deviation, volatility. But the impact or the ethical standards that a company maintains are more qualitative than quantitative and even then, it's very difficult to see where they are on a spectrum, because measurement of this nature is difficult.

Fifty Shades of Green

I call it the Fifty Shades of Green issue – where exactly do companies sit on these various measures and how do we measure them? Judgement on measurement is highly subjective and relies on qualitative rather than quantitative analysis. There is no standard definition of what ESG actually is, and each factor is on a scale.

What is an acceptable achievement for one investor may be unacceptable to another, and priorities will vary between E, S & G. And, of course, these are just three letters in the complex and ill-defined alphabet soup of different definitions and measurement systems.

To some extent, it's up to individuals to decide, from an ethical perspective, what they're okay or not okay with investing in. The 'Does harm' graphic below shows whether an investment is neutral, positive or negative.

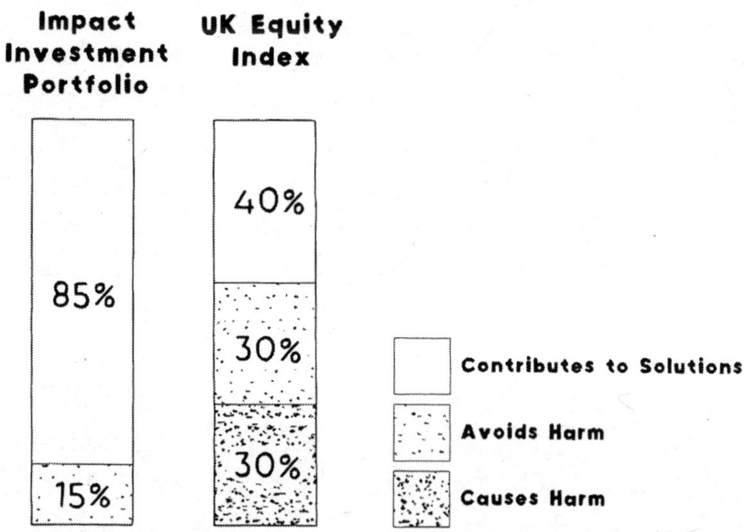

Figure 5

When looking at the FTSE 100 index, about a third of the companies could be deemed harmful for people and the planet. When reviewing the typical impact investment, 85% on the bar chart show positive, with 15% neutral and 0% negative.

Along with other high-conviction investors, Path Financial encourages more transparency, higher standards and better regulation for the measurement of impact. One thing I think will help significantly in this arena is competition. Once we've got some recognised metrics to measure company performance, competition and transparency, we'll be able to make comparisons, which will naturally lead to better accountability.

The Current Measures

Net-zero declaration is one, in terms of when companies are planning to reduce their carbon emissions to zero. But, of course, it's easy to make a declaration, and not so easy to fulfil it. Just ask anyone who's said "No problem, I'll just lose a stone before my summer holidays." So the question is, how credible is the declaration? It's all very well for a company to produce a climate or sustainability report, but it's a different matter producing a good and truthful one, much less one which can be compared to others. We still lack standards to assess the credibility of net-zero claims, as we do with carbon neutrality or alignment with the United Nations sustainable development goals, which we'll look at shortly. The bottom line is that without a standard in place, it's impossible to measure accurately.

Consumers want to make positive choices around their investments. Pressure groups such as Make My Money Matter, ShareAction and Pensions For Purpose are all very welcome since they give consumers a voice and hold companies accountable to ever-higher and more transparent measures.

Although it is difficult, progress is being made. Who would have thought that Larry Fink, the leader of BlackRock, one of the biggest fund managers in the world, would urge business leaders to consider their environmental impact?

Net Zero and Carbon Neutral

At a country level, out of the 195 recognised countries in the world, only around 135 have made a pledge to be carbon neutral. Of these, about 90% appear to have a target of 2050 – though unfortunately this is mainly due to their membership of the Carbon Neutrality Coalition,[9] which states this ambition – but it leaves countries' individual commitments up to them. In reality, less than half of the 135 countries have made a commitment. Far fewer have aligned their government policy with any realistic prospect of meeting the targets. To their credit, the UK is one of those to have enshrined their commitment in law. Others include Denmark, France, Hungary, New Zealand and Sweden.

We do have a couple of early winners in the "race" to net zero: Suriname and Bhutan were first across the line before COP26 and make quite valid claims to be carbon negative. We might also add Benin, Cambodia, Gabon, Guinea-Bissau, Guyana, Liberia and Madagascar, many of which are relatively undeveloped and/or have heavy forest cover. Other

9 https://carbon-neutrality.global/

countries will have to work very hard to ever reach net zero. Leading the pack in terms of bigger countries with ambitious targets are Uruguay (2030), Finland (2035), Austria and Iceland (2040), and Germany and Sweden (2045).

Many oil-producing countries and the larger emitters have 2060 as a target. India, at 2070, has propelled it so far into the future it doesn't have to worry about accountability for a couple of generations. Unfortunately, by then, it will be too late – India has one of the coastlines most vulnerable to rising sea levels. And it will be far, far too late for nearby regions like Sundarbans. 11% of Bangladesh is estimated to be under water by 2050.[10] In investment circles, we're used to speaking about emerging markets, while, tragically, we should really be talking in terms of submerging markets.

Politicians are, of course, happy to boot the problem into the long grass since they know it won't be their own re-election prospects that will be judged. *No, that's a problem for the next incumbent.* They are quite safe – even in setting a reasonably ambitious target, as long as it's two or three decades away, they'll be collecting their pension and long-forgotten.

As with governments, companies also are rather short-termist in their thinking, and prone to more devious and cynical reporting of targets and achievements. When a company like Shell sets a net-zero

10 https://www.climaterealityproject.org/blog/how-climate-crisis-impacting-bangladesh

target date of 2050, this must at best be, ahem, ambitious. Greenpeace was somewhat more trenchant in its view, describing it as "grotesque ... and delusional".[11]

2021 Oxfam report *Tightening the Net* pointed out that many companies are relying on unproven and as-yet-uninvented carbon capture strategies that will offset a business-as-usual level of emissions. To put this into perspective, to fulfil their net-zero promises, BP, Eni, Shell and Total would require them to forest an area twice the size of the UK to achieve net zero by 2050. That would include planting all the cities, lakes and mountain areas where trees won't even grow, as well as farmland. In fact, the report concludes that, to have a chance of success, tree planting would have to be undertaken on a scale equivalent to all the farmland in the world. The charity concludes that net-zero targets are often a "greenwashing" exercise.

Measurable Data

Greenhouse Gas (GHG) Accounting, or Carbon Accounting, refers to the attempt to measure how much carbon dioxide equivalent (CO2e) an organisation emits. The term first appeared in the Greenhouse Gas Protocol[12] (a partnership between the World Business Council for Sustainable Development (WBCSD) and the

11 https://www.greenpeace.org.uk/news/shells-net-zero-plan-grotesque-and-delusional
12 https://ghgprotocol.org/

World Resources Institute (WRI)) and has three scopes, which are now the basis for mandatory GHG reporting for around 1,100 UK-listed companies.

Scope 1 covers the emissions a company makes directly from sources it owns or controls – for example running its vehicles, boilers, furnaces, and any other type of fuel combustion.

Scope 2 covers indirect GHG emissions, principally from purchased resources such as electricity, heat or cooling. That is to say, the emissions are generated not on the company's sites but on those of a third party – for example, an electricity power station.

Scope 3 covers all other indirect emissions from the company's supply chain, both upstream (suppliers) and downstream (distribution). Scope 3 emissions can account for 90% or more of a company's emissions, including purchased goods and services, transport and distribution, employee commuting, business travel, waste, and eventual disposal of products. Difficult as Scope 3 emissions are to pin down, they are important. Compare, if you will, the Scope 1 and 2 scores involved in building a small boat and a wind turbine. They might be very similar in terms of manufacturing process emissions, and based on these measures alone, you might conclude the environmental harm to be similar. But in their lifetime usage – as measured by Scope 3 – one will spend most of its life burning marine diesel with a big Scope 3 score, whereas the other will spend most of its life creating clean, renewable energy with a negative Scope 3 score.

It seems to be widely accepted that there are flaws in the GHG reporting. It's felt that a tiny minority of companies report emissions completely and that data quality is poor. There is likely a lot of double-counting of Scope 3 emissions when a particular process is allocated to many parties in the supply chain. Nonetheless, this is the type of reporting standard we need and which can be refined. The International Organization for Standardization (ISO) has introduced standards for greenhouse gas accounting under ISO 14064, and there is co-operation between the ISO and other reporting bodies to ensure more consistent standards be applied in a complementary way.

Impact Investment

There are three observable attributes that distinguish impact investments from other investments:

- They must have an intent to achieve a social and/or environmental goal through their investment.
- They need a credible narrative of how the actions of the impact investment will achieve their goals.
- They've got a system of measurement in place that links intent, contribution and improvement of the investment.

The ABC Method

Another way of thinking about impact investment would be to use the ABC method discussed earlier:

A – Avoid harm
B – Benefit stakeholders
C – Contribute to solutions

A lot of financial data is recorded, but impact data less so. And what has been recorded is used for risk measurement of investing in a particular stock, depending on the risks that present themselves and the consciousness of the risks associated with the company in question. By having better metrics, we can better predict companies' financial success and highlight more opportunities.

A more recent and welcome development is the Task Force on Climate-related Financial Disclosures (TCFD), established in 2015 by the G20 Financial Stability Board, which requires companies to sign up to internationally agreed standards on disclosures relating to governance, strategy and risk management.[13] The aim is to have consistent and comparable metrics across all sectors, specific metrics for the most carbon-intense sectors, and to present the potential impact of the risks and opportunities through financial reporting. The TCFD was charged with developing recommendations for voluntary standards, but ones which were consistent,

13 https://www.fsb.org/

comparable, reliable and clear so that investors, lenders and insurers – other stakeholders who need to manage these risks – had the information to hand. The UK is leading the way with the TCFD as the first country to make the disclosures mandatory. This requirement will start in 2025, but some companies will report earlier.

The EU Sustainable Finance Disclosure Regulation (SFDR)

The EU SFDR was introduced to help investors by requiring investment managers to provide more transparency on the characteristics of investments that are promoted as having environmental or social benefits. There are currently three relevant articles, which the SFDR introduced, the idea being that investors can instantly see what category any proposed investment falls into and can make consumer choices accordingly:

- Article 6 – funds that rarely integrate sustainability into the investment process. They will still be allowed to be sold in the EU, but to all intents and purposes, this labels them as non-sustainable.
- Article 8 – broadly, funds that are ESG-related or ethical, also known as "environmentally and socially promoting". We might call these "light green".

- Article 9 – products that claim to be positive impact, also known as "products targeting sustainable investments". We might call these "dark green".

This is an encouraging development as it's the first time we've had standards in the public domain that can hold funds and fund managers to account by definition, testing and comparison.

The United Nations Sustainable Development Goals (SDGs)

As described on their website: 'The Sustainable Development Goals are the blueprint to achieve a better and more sustainable future for all.[14] They address the global challenges we face, including poverty, inequality, climate change, environmental degradation, peace, and justice.'

They comprise 17 interlinked goals:

1. No Poverty
2. Zero Hunger
3. Good Health and Well-being
4. Quality Education
5. Gender Equality
6. Clean Water and Sanitation
7. Affordable and Clean Energy
8. Decent Work and Economic Growth
9. Industry, Innovation and Infrastructure

14 https://www.un.org/sustainabledevelopment/sustainable-development-goals/

10. Reduced Inequality
11. Sustainable Cities and Communities
12. Responsible Consumption and Production
13. Climate Action
14. Life Below Water
15. Life On Land
16. Peace, Justice, and Strong Institutions
17. Partnerships for the Goals

If we assume the SDGs are the solution, then we can map investments to them. If a company's products and services are a contributor to these solutions, then we have the basis for a positive impact measurement. Having a methodology for mapping companies, and hence funds, to the SDGs is currently a very labour-intensive and manual process. Because of the nuance, subtlety, spin and greenwash that abound, it takes analysts time and skill to assess. Nonetheless, it is a useful and consistent framework. Companies' core products and services can be assessed and attributed positively or negatively to one or more of the SDGs in terms of what has already been achieved. This goes much further than most other methods, which tend to only take intentionality into account.

Going Forward

Some ratings agencies now judge funds on ESG metrics, which is another positive development, and they have developed a scoring mechanism for how "sustainable" a particular fund is. The snag is it relies on self-reported information and what we can glean from artificial intelligence (AI), and that data is still sparse.

In reporting Scope 1, 2 and 3 emissions, emerging best practice would define a net-zero objective with clear short-term and longer-term milestones, and publish the internal metrics companies use to monitor their own progress, gauge success, and look at the key results areas and their own measurements. They would evaluate board-level governance and embed the ESG and what's known as "impact metrics" in their executive compensation schemes. I hope that over time company governance will be measured by quality, transparency and authenticity. And those with better reporting standards and more honest appraisals will be deemed leaders – and more investible.

Earlier, we speculated how companies with a clear "why" at the heart of what they do will be more investible. And so it is, with measurement, we view successful company leadership as imparting a sense of purpose. It has a clear action in pursuit of the objective, and values-based leaders will create a more enthusiastic uptake of the standards they're trying to achieve towards a common goal. Consumers get behind that type of authenticity. It's a win-win because, by operating in this holistic way, everyone will be rewarded for their efforts towards achieving the measurements. For this to become the normal way of doing things, we must tie employee financial incentives to profit achieved sustainably through meeting these standards.

I'm optimistic the quality of data will improve, but meanwhile, a thorough analysis of performance requires a high level of manual intervention. We're not remotely near the point where there's enough information in the public domain for comparisons to be made, so it's still a specialist job, which is why most fund and portfolio managers rely on manual analysis. It's as unsophisticated as starting with what we call a sniff test, which looks at what individual companies are doing and requires heavy research to find a reliable degree of measurement.

In conclusion, we still only have crude measures in place such as greenhouse gas emissions, net-zero declarations and, to some extent, mapping of the degrees of warming generated by company activities. We need to see measures around diversity and gender balance on company boards. We need more measures related to climate change, and investors with other, more granular, interests. Vegan investors, for example, will want to know how aligned the companies they're investing in comply with their values and ethics. As measurement develops, we can create this more granular data and have more clarity around the impact companies are making, which will allow for greater consumer choice.

CHAPTER 6

ALIGNING YOUR INVESTMENTS WITH YOUR VALUES

There is so much more to consider than a positive return on investment when choosing where to invest your funds and pension. Aligning your values and ethics with your investments takes more effort than expecting intermediaries, funds or institutions to do the right thing. Whether consciously or not, financial advisers are not all equal when it comes to green investments, and it is up to us to educate ourselves so we know where our money is going.

Greenwashing

"Greenwashing" was coined in the 1980s by environmentalist Jay Westerveld, who objected to the new practice of hoteliers asking their guests to only leave the towels they wanted washed in the bathtub and to consider the impact on the environment of requesting freshly laundered towels every day. This is clever because it subtly places the onus on the hotel guest to do the right thing, and the new normal becomes not to provide fresh towels as part of their service. He saw this as a ploy to reduce hotels' service and laundry costs and said there was nothing to suggest they cared about the environmental footprint caused by the excessive laundering of the towels. The term greenwashing is modelled on "whitewashing", which is an attempt to conceal the dirty truth. It's also sometimes referred to as "green sheen". What we're talking about is the spin advertising agencies put on things. Greenwashing seeks to emphasise the "green" aspects of a company or organisation and divert attention from what's going on behind the scenes.

You might recall some controversy with McDonald's in 2019, when they introduced paper straws since they appeared to be more eco-friendly than plastic ones. The problem was, not only did this involve cutting down trees and using energy to make the paper, but the straws were, ahem, not recyclable. Oops – bigger environmental footprint for a similarly bad outcome to before.

You only need to walk down any supermarket aisle, or indeed a petrol forecourt, to see examples of eco-spin. Nestlé claims that, by 2025, all of its plastic bottles will be made from recyclable plastic. Which, when you say it fast, sounds quite good. But the practical real-world outcome is that, rather than being recycled, they'll no doubt end up in our oceans or landfill. Or worse, be incinerated.

Greenwashing shifts attention away from the bad onto whatever good there may be – even if it's tenuous. The example I rather enjoy using is, going to market with the claim that butter is 20% fat-free!

Another example would be a brand promoting their margarine or butter as vegan but the label listing palm oil as one of its ingredients. While it may technically be vegan, palm oil is an ingredient vegans avoid because harvesting it typically has a destructive impact on the environment – deforestation – and particularly on orangutans. It's widely used because of its versatility. So, it's easy to get caught out and think something's a sustainably produced product just because it's vegan. Some palm oil is certified sustainable, but even this is controversial because deforestation occurs through the production of much palm oil.[15]

As with brands and products, certain funds and fund managers portray their offerings as greener than they are to be able to sell them as green, even when they're not. The rise of greenwashing paired with ineffective regulation contributes to consumer scepticism of green claims, and it diminishes the power of the consumer to drive companies towards greener processes and business operations. Many

15 https://www.greenpeace.org.uk/news/5-problems-with-sustainable-palm-oil/

corporations use greenwashing to improve public perception of their brands, and complex corporate structures make it even more complicated to spot because they have experts casting a green aura on things. Without external monitoring and verification, the greenwashing strategy amounts to posturing and deception, where a company portrays themselves as behaving responsibly, and adopting a sustainable development vision. To be greener, a company may have to change its culture and integrate sustainable development into its commercial activities.

Greenwashing works in the same way as any type of spin brands have traditionally used to influence people to buy their products or invest in their services. Given the current attention on sustainable living and climate change, all eyes are on green. Greenwashing is virtue signalling for companies and individuals who preach their green values on social media about how they're saving the planet (the inference being they're virtuous), and then hire a private jet to fly to a climate conference. It's the age-old 'do as I say, not as I do'.

The Seven Sins of Greenwashing

A study called The Seven Sins of Greenwashing discovered 95% of consumer products claiming to be green had committed at least one of the seven sins.[16]

16 https://www.ul.com/insights/sins-greenwashing

Here's a summary of the sins:

- **The first sin** is a hidden trade-off – the claim that a product is green, based on a narrow set of attributes, without paying attention to other environmental issues.
- **The second sin** is not showing proof of a claim that cannot be substantiated by easily accessible information.
- **The third sin** is vagueness – a claim that's poorly defined or so broad it has no clear meaning and can be misunderstood by the consumer.
- **The fourth sin** is worshipping false labels – a claim that through words or images gives the impression a third-party endorsement exists for a product when it doesn't.
- **The fifth sin** is irrelevance – a claim that may be truthful but which isn't relevant to consumers seeking products that don't harm the environment.
- **Sin number six** is the lesser of two evils – a claim that may be true but which aims to distract consumers from the environmental impact.
- **Sin number seven** is fibbing – this is about making false environmental claims and maybe stating a product is certified by a recognised organisation when it isn't.

It's important we understand where a particular spin is being put on things. There's also the question of whether you avoid an investment – let's say divestment – or whether you engage as a shareholder. I see this as being clear about your boundaries. When considering whether an investment aligns with your values and ethics, ask yourself whether you are okay with this investment. When we are committed to aligning our values with our investments, we have to have a boundary around what we're prepared to invest in and what opportunities we're willing to decline. When it comes to fossil fuels, for example, my ethos is that we don't engage with that type of investment at all and so my clients' investments reflect that. They can be confident their money is only working for funds and initiatives that to my knowledge support people and the planet.

This is the straightforward way to remove any conflict with your value system and is how my company operates. There's a contrary view, where you might choose to invest in companies that need to change so that your voice is heard and your vote as a shareholder is counted. This is the helping-to-create-change-from-the-inside approach. For me, this is another method of greenwashing. When an investor takes this route, they can find themselves compromised – it's all too easy to use it as an excuse to own a share because the investment potentially has a high-growth prospect or a big dividend.

As in all things, only you know what the right

approach is for you, and you must trust your values. I see engaging with a fossil fuel company like being in an abusive relationship. To be safe, you must exit the relationship immediately until such time, if ever, the person moderates their behaviour. You can't negotiate from within, but it's tempting to make excuses for them because you want them to be what you know they could be.

In conclusion, greenwashing is when companies, brands and organisations make unsubstantiated claims to deceive consumers into believing their products are environmentally friendly. Although some of the environmental claims might be partially true, they typically exaggerate the benefits or take your attention away from what they don't want you to know. We've all seen the headlines in the media – journalists and publications have their own political viewpoints and agendas, so they're inherently biased. The same event can sound completely different depending on the chosen headline, because the journalist will have projected the negative or the positive angle from their own viewpoint. It's just as easy to be fooled by greenwashing spin as it is media spin.

Becoming a Green Champion

To be champions of accurate metrics, we must confront greenwashing claims by presenting our investors with more reliable data and looking at ways to verify the claims. There isn't currently an organisation that monitors greenwashing claims, so it's up to investors to analyse the data. For this reason, it's even more important to choose your financial adviser or money manager wisely. While they may have an excellent track record of creating a positive return on investment, the goalposts have moved. In fact, the whole playing field has moved. If we want to invest in environmentally positive funds, it's critical to align ourselves with professionals who take more than profit into account.

If we look at the entire universe of investments, environmental, social and governance factors are not typically considered. The vast minority of funds have ESG attributes. If we're looking at environmental, social and governance, I estimate only about 10% of advisers evaluate how green an investment is.

Choosing Your Financial Adviser

For those committed to aligning their values with their investments, the big question is, what does your financial adviser consider when recommending investments? Some have a broad brush ESG overlay, but how do they define E, S and G? Is the investment light green or dark green? (How green is it?) If they align themselves with light-green investments, they might still recommend investing in an oil company, and say they're moving towards a more environmentally friendly process, as in the earlier example. The question would be, is that true? Are they an oil company just intent on selling more oil or are they an energy company intent on changing their behaviour to produce a new environmentally positive strategy? A financial adviser who only invests in dark-green funds wouldn't invest in fossil fuel companies. Another aspect to consider is how they assess impact. Does the financial adviser seek to exclude the obviously negative, but also look at including positive elements in their clients' portfolios?

In Part Two, we will look at practical tips and ideas for your financial planning so you can create or develop your ethical pension and investments.

PART TWO

CHAPTER 7

INTRODUCTION TO FINANCIAL PLANNING

We've talked about the concept of impact investment and aligning investments with your values. That is something I recommend you do once you've thought about what financial independence or financial security means for you, and what a financial management programme might look like. Of course, that is much easier said than done and it can be rather a taboo subject, especially in the UK, so a little guidance is extremely helpful. With that in mind, this part of the book will look at the basics of practical financial planning.

A long time ago, when I first started in this business, my mentors taught me that people are going to live too long, die too soon or get sick in the meantime, and that is the reality for the majority of us. Beyond that, financial planning is thinking about things like investment management for accumulated wealth, inheritance tax management, legacy planning and philanthropy. First, let's look at the live too long, die too soon, get sick in the meantime scenarios, one by one.

Live Too Long

This is the risk of outliving your money. To avoid this, the emphasis is on amassing enough money during what we call the accumulation phase, or the working phase of life, to have sufficient funds to meet lifestyle expenses in the decumulation phase, or retirement. We will explore this in later chapters.

Die Too Soon

What does dying too soon mean in financial planning terms? Well, that means dying before you've accumulated sufficient wealth. For a single person, that's not necessarily a problem, but for someone with financial responsibilities, and a family to care for, if you don't live long enough to build up sufficient assets, then where will the money come from if you die? This is where we hear harrowing stories about spouses and their children being left penniless – even homeless – after the premature death of the primary income provider. It's because of potential tragedies like this that people consider taking out life insurance. So, this is contingency planning to create money for dying too soon.

Get Sick in the Meantime

In this scenario, it might mean you can't work because of sickness or disability, or even if you can, you might be advised on medical grounds that you shouldn't. Let's say you had a heart attack, and the doctor tells you not to work again, but you've got a mortgage to pay. If you had prepared for the worst and insured yourself against adversity by arranging critical illness insurance or income protection insurance, you'd be covered for such an eventuality and could pay the debt off and have an income provided by the insurance.

Most people have considerable worries and concerns around these three scenarios, or at least they would if they stopped to think about them. They all speak to the question of 'how much is enough?' It has been my experience that virtually no one has the right types and amount of coverage and that people tend to adopt an "ostrich posture".

We might also think about situations where there is already "more than enough" – family wealth, large inheritance, business sale, lottery win, or a sum of money available for investment. As wonderful as it may sound, people are often apprehensive about this. Inexperience can make people feel too nervous to invest in the way they should to manage their money well. There's anxiety about making your money last, relative to inflation. And then, of course, there's the fact that, when you pass away, the government taxes your estate at a high percentage. At the time of writing, inheritance tax sits at 40%.

Key Areas

This is an overview of the key areas to consider – the basics of financial planning:

- What happens if you live too long?
- What happens if you die too soon?
- What happens if you get sick in the meantime?
- How do you get superior investment returns and stay ahead of inflation?
- How do you pass the inheritance to your family or causes you care about without too big a deduction?

Let's assume we're talking about the timeline of the average person. For this exercise, it doesn't really matter where you are on that line. To figure out how much money you need, I advise you take into account just four variables.

The Four Variables

- How much do you intend to spend every year of the rest of your life?
- How long are you going to live?
- What investment return will you get?
- What will the rate of inflation be?

If you knew the answer to these four questions, financial planning would be extremely straightforward. The problem is, generally speaking, nobody can know the answers to all these questions. And these questions are typically difficult to ask as well as answer. People try not to think about life expectancy or discuss their inevitable death. They have vague concerns, and the topic is awkward to confront. A good financial planner will sit you down and talk you through each of the following areas in a professional and caring manner and help you plan accordingly.

Let's touch on the basics of the four variables, in this introductory chapter.

Life Expectancy

The average UK citizen lives until the age of 81.[17] Obviously, some people will live longer, some will die sooner, and some will have health issues. A sensible plan will factor in a useful average. For a couple, the chance of one of them making it to later life is that much greater.

The statistical average is 81. But if you're already 81, then the government actuarial tables will tell you that you can expect another nine years.[18] The life expectancy for a 90-year-old is 95. So, the longer you live, the longer you're predicted to live.

It's interesting to note that life expectancy in the

17 https://www.google.com/search?q=average+life+expectancy+uk
18 https://www.ssa.gov/oact/STATS/table4c6.html

UK seems to have plateaued recently, if not dropped slightly. It's a sad fact that obesity and diabetes, to name two factors, are much more influential now and are taking their toll more than they used to. Some health issues are random and come from out of the blue. Others are more lifestyle-related. The World Health Organization reckons three times as many people now die from obesity as they do from malnutrition.[19]

When we're talking about passing assets on to family, the timeline could be very long indeed, and investment returns are complicated to figure out. A good plan will look at several assumptions about time periods and inflation projections.

Lifetime Spending

How much you spend over a certain number of years is also incredibly difficult to predict. Certainly, while you're earning money or running a business or have income from investment, your income will be relatively stable. And most people have their expenses pegged at something just under their income level. But in retirement, it could be radically different. Your early retirement years will be when you're at your most active and likely to have higher expenditure needs. It's a curious thing that the Civil Service pension scheme (the gold standard of pensions) assumes an income of two-thirds of pre-retirement income as a maximum. While this might be a dream for many, it's quite likely you'll

19 https://www.who.int/news-room/fact-sheets/detail/malnutrition

want to have an even higher disposable income at this time to fulfil the bucket-list activities and experiences you didn't have time to pursue when you were working. As we approach more advanced old age and slow down and don't travel as much, our income needs tend to *reduce* dramatically. Expenditure may drop in later life. On the other hand, if you had to go into long-term care, expenses would *shoot up* dramatically, so it's all rather difficult to foresee, which is why so many people avoid tackling it, and don't create a solid financial plan.

You may have heard it said that most people spend longer thinking about their annual holiday than they do their lifetime's income and financial plan. I've found this to be broadly true, for the reasons we talked about earlier: lack of knowing how to go about it, lack of knowing the questions to ask, general nervousness, and the ostrich effect of confronting something difficult.

In summary, we break financial planning down into the accumulation and the decumulation phases. The accumulation phase, for many people, is about *using your life to make your money*. I think it's very important at every stage of the process that you think about how you are going to *use your money to make your life*. With our clients, we get to the point where we discuss what financial independence looks like for them. For those who already have large, accumulated savings or wealth, there might be other considerations such as trust, estate planning and philanthropy. Going back to Maslow, the more our basic needs are fulfilled, the more we are motivated to pursue higher-level needs. From this principle, he concludes that we fulfil the fullest or highest extent of human satisfaction by giving ourselves to something beyond ourselves, spiritually or altruistically, say.

I recommend asking yourself these five questions:

- What is the life you want to live?
- How much will it cost?
- Where will that income come from?
- How will you go about accumulating that money in the first place?
- Where and how will you invest it?

These are some of the practical aspects and questions we're going to address together in the rest of this book.

Human existence is about striving for happiness, but happiness comes from having a sense of purpose and a sense of direction. When you reach the point of financial independence, it can be quite challenging to answer these questions because happiness is but a feeling and impossible to correlate to a specific sum of money. Certainly, having more money can make life easier and opens choices that are closed without the funds to finance them. As the saying goes, 'I've been poor and I've been rich and believe me, rich is better!' Recognising how much is enough is the key.

I vaguely remember a survey from my early days in the industry which sought to elicit an answer to 'how much is enough?' An extensive group of people were interviewed, from refuse collectors to barristers, and, in fact, an answer did emerge. The amount needed in almost every case was double what they already had. This chasing-the-pot-of-gold-at-the-end-of-the-rainbow approach leads to undue anxiety and overlong working careers, whereas a clear understanding of what's important can lead to more happiness and a much more well-defined plan. Not easy. But this is an area where a skilled financial planner will be a valuable counsellor.

Creating a Plan

It is possible to factor the four key variables of financial planning into a sophisticated spreadsheet and have a crack at answering the associated questions and modelling financial outcomes. If you're the sort of person who has a fondness for spreadsheets and numbers, then weeks of fun could be had experimenting with the calculations. Alternatively, if that's not your idea of fun, you could choose to work with an adviser, who would probably have some off-the-peg tools to allow you to circumvent the hard work. If you go down the do-it-yourself route, it will be cheaper upfront, but it may cost you more in the long run, depending on your understanding of financial planning. Not only do you have to think about the four key variables, but you must figure out what your investment management proposition will look like. It's enough of a challenge identifying the "known unknowns" (things you know you don't know), which is all about identifying your knowledge gap on things like financial products, investment management and asset allocation. But what about the "unknown unknowns" (things that you don't know that you don't know) – complex tax rules, reliefs, insurance products and actuarial life expectancy?

Caring about the impact your money has adds another dimension of complexity to your plan. I often say to people who want to save a few quid by doing it themselves, there are lots of things you can do yourself and save money on, and many of them might be quite enjoyable. Others not necessarily so. Take dentistry – conceivably, you could attempt it on your own, but you'd do so at your peril ...

This is the school of thought about working with a professional adviser. That said, a lot of financial advisers have the reputation of putting themselves ahead of their clients. Knowing who to take advice from is important. Some advisers will try to prove how clever they are by using jargon and technicalities, but then bamboozle their clients. I think financial planning is an area where you are best to take advice, but it's wise to choose your adviser carefully. I recommend you work with someone who puts you at the centre of your financial plan, takes your values into account, and asks you how you want to use your money to create and fund your lifestyle. Someone who will discuss your views on ethical issues and the impact your money can have.

Find a financial adviser who explains things as simply as possible. It was Einstein (him again!) who said we should "make things as simple as possible, but no simpler". That is a philosophy to which I adhere. We don't need to know precisely how our car works, if it gets us from A to B. And it's a bit like that with financial planning. You don't need to know all the technicalities. As long as the adviser is competent, they don't need to explain every minute detail to the client. A poor adviser will showboat how much they know but leave you confused and possibly not listened to. I've noticed that clients *don't care how much you know* as much as wanting to *know how much you care*.

Later, I will share specific strategies, hints and tips, but here is an overview to complete this chapter.

Most investments seek to do two things: produce an income and/or produce a capital gain. In my experience, all *value-able* investments are easier to value when you know the income they produce, because you can attribute an income multiple to get to the value of the asset. This is easy for property investment. You buy a property, get a tenant, and that gives you a rent of X pounds per annum. People like property investment because it's quite a simple concept to understand. It also has commodity or market value, which is to say, a street of 40 identical houses will all more or less have the same value depending on market conditions.

The capital value of most assets is a multiple of the income they generate. Let's say you have a property generating £10,000 a year of rent. Typically, the capital value of that asset would be 6 to 25 times the rent it could predictably generate.

Six times might be something like a lock-up shop or garage in a poor part of town, where the quality of the income stream might be variable. You might get gaps in the income and not have a tenant for a while. On the higher end, you might invest in a tip-top office building or a luxury apartment with a high capital value. The rent would be constrained by what people can afford to pay, but it would be a valuable asset, trading on a high multiple of the yield it could achieve. So, property is easy to understand as an asset; that is, the rent concept is simple. You can actually touch your investment. It's a good hedge against inflation because values – rent and prices – go up as economic conditions dictate. And another massive virtue of property investment is that you can borrow to make a bigger investment than you otherwise could. It's about the only investment asset type where you get to use this leverage. The power of OPM (other people's money) can ratchet up gains significantly in a rising market (or wipe you out in a falling market). On the downside, property has massive transaction costs, is illiquid and comes in one-unit sizes which tend to be very large. Plus, it gets caught by all the major personal taxes.

Banks will lend you money to invest in property in such a way that they won't give you money to invest in anything else. And that's great because with an 80% mortgage, for example, for every pound you put into a deal, you're getting £4 of other people's money. Now the beauty of that is, if the property you purchase doubles, then you've made a return of 500% on the contribution you made to the deal.

Let's say you invest £100,000 and get a £400,000 loan on a £500,000 property. Over time, it doubles in value to £1 million, you pay the bank back, and you're left with £600,000, which is a huge return. But this can also be a double-edged sword, which we tend to forget about. If the property halves in value, then you wipe out all your capital and the bank can come after you for the difference. Leverage is great when you do well, but it can be savage when you do badly. There are some tremendous positives around property investment, which we mentioned in the previous chapter, but there are also negatives to consider.

Property Investment Negatives

- They come in big single units.
- You can't sell just a few bricks of a property to take advantage of a capital gain tax allowance. It's all or nothing in any tax year.
- Property is subject to higher rates of income tax, but with limited breaks on tax relief.
- You will pay capital gains tax at a higher rate than on stocks and shares.
- Any debt you've got is limited in terms of what you can offset against profit.

- It will be in your estate for inheritance tax purposes.
- It has a special acquisition tax all of its own – Stamp Duty Land Tax (SDLT) – which means there's often a major cost to acquire it.
- You might have to pay business rates on a commercial property if you don't have a tenant to pay it. A double whammy: no income and an extra tax burden, just to rub salt into the wound.
- From a tax efficiency point of view, property investment is poor.
- You have the risk of not finding a tenant, for example if they don't pay, or the neighbourhood goes into decline.
- It's an illiquid asset that takes a long time to sell.
- It's generally not particularly positive impact.

On the maintenance side, things tend to go wrong with property at the most inopportune times. The one thing you can say about an ISA is that its toilet won't get blocked on a Sunday afternoon. So be careful when investing in property not to create a job for yourself.

If we compare that to stocks and shares investing, which people get quite nervous about, and don't particularly understand, the same two components exist. To recap Chapter 4, established companies make a profit, and the profit is paid out to shareholders as a dividend income. The dividend will vary from zero and be anything up to 8 or 9%. Let's think of the dividend income as being like the rent for the property. The shares will trade on a multiple, again depending on the quality of the business, ranging from anything from three up to one hundred times. Amazon trades on a very high multiple of earnings, and pretty much always has, because the market thinks there's a huge amount of growth there. Stocks and shares are relatively straightforward if you think about them in terms of property investment. There's an income element and, hopefully, there's some capital growth too.

Unlike property, however, shares are highly liquid – there is always a value in the market for listed shares, which is a benefit. You can buy and sell them daily. Also, their boilers don't explode, and their roofs don't need replacing, so they're a lot easier to look after in many ways. Shares and funds come in very small unit sizes, so you can sell a part of your holding. Unlike property, where it's all or nothing. There are many instances where this is useful. Managing tax allowances is one. Or, if you double your investment with shares, you can sell half, recoup your original investment and then have a free ride with the remainder. You have de-risked your original stake and, in a sense, who cares what happens to the amount you have left – you can risk keeping it invested to see where it might end up. Shares can be held in tax-efficient wrappers, as we will go on to see. A penny saved is a penny earned, as they say, so avoiding tax is akin to achieving a higher investment return.

The Principles of Wealth Creation

If you need to work for a living, and you've got a lifestyle cost of **X** pounds per annum, you need to earn **X** pounds per year after tax. For every pound of investment income you receive, that is another pound of income you don't need to earn. So, in terms of younger readers thinking about accumulating a pot, even a pound of income from an invested asset is a pound you don't need to earn. Do this and you'll be starting the first steps on your journey to financial independence. A thousand pounds from passive investments is another thousand pounds you don't need to earn. The faster you can transition from having to sell your labour to meet your lifestyle costs and replace it with investments which work for you, the better.

This principle is the basis of Robert Kiyosaki's very good and readable book *Rich Dad Poor Dad*. This should be required reading for anyone aspiring to make a DIY financial plan, even if it is skewed very much towards property investment.

> **You can invest every pound you earn, but don't *need* to earn.**

By doing this you get an exponential curve, where the more passive income you've got, the less you need to earn, because your financial independence is closer. Thus, you can invest more of your "excess" income or take more leisure time.

You can see the exponential effect on the chart below. If you want to achieve financial independence, it's critical to understand that if you start accumulating invested assets at a young age, you'll give yourself a great deal of time to accumulate wealth.

The eighth wonder of the world is compound interest. As you can see on the chart, there's a curve, which goes up at the far end of the timeline. The biggest gains are made at the end as you earn interest not only on the principal invested but on the interest created too. The interest on the interest on the interest later dwarfs the small amount earned at the start. This means that if you do the hard yards at the start, then you'll reap the rewards of the tremendous growth on

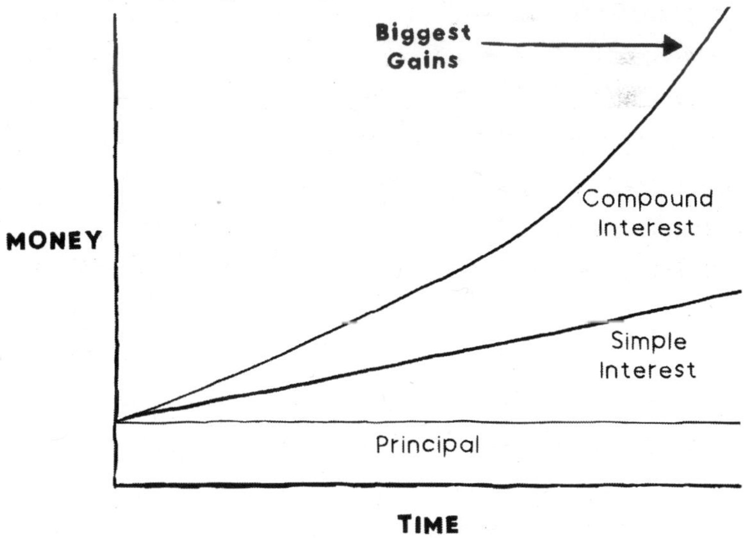

Figure 6

the early money invested. If you start setting aside savings and investments from an early age, you'll build up an impregnably large portfolio that will look after you financially for the rest of your life. (More of this in Chapter 8.)

> *Compound interest is the eighth wonder of the world. He who understands it earns it; he who does not pays it* – Albert Einstein.

Market Timing

People get terribly absorbed in timing when it comes to stock market investment. *Yes, but I want to buy at the bottom of the market.* There are only two problems with that. Firstly, no one rings a bell to tell you the market has reached the bottom. You simply cannot know in advance when that will be. Secondly, the bottom of the market usually comes when there is the biggest fear and trepidation that the future of the economy and the market looks very worrying. These are precisely the conditions which make it extremely difficult to be brave enough to step in where everyone else fears to tread. *The stock market is the only market where people don't buy when there is a sale on,* I've heard said.

'Buy on the sound of cannon and sell on the sound of trumpets' is a great adage. Coined in 1810 and attributed to Nathan Rothschild, it essentially means, if you buy when there is bad news and when fear abounds, it will likely prove to be a lower point in the market and a good time to buy. Conversely, the market and its prices will be most exuberant and high when things seem to be going well – that is a good time to sell, ahead of the next downturn.

This is all very well in theory but quite hard to implement given human nature. Most amateur investors wait until the market has had a good run before they prepare to take the plunge and invest. After months or years of rising markets, two things happen. One is that despite their fear of volatility, they convince themselves this time it's different, and that a good run proves markets are reliable and go up after all. Secondly, FOMO (fear of missing out) kicks in – and after such a good run, they'd hate to miss out. This is often followed by a period of negative news

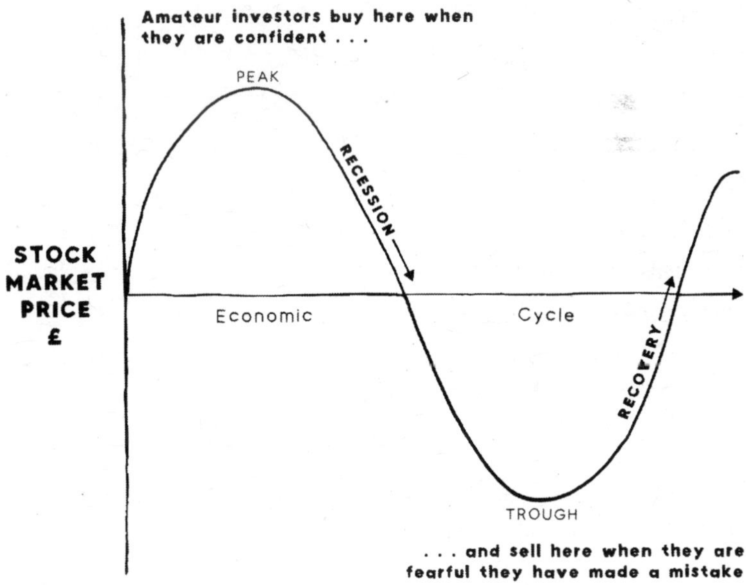

Figure 7

and the market starting to fall. Our amateur investor starts to look at their portfolio and sees it's becoming worth less and less as the days and weeks roll by. After convincing themselves that financial markets will never recover, they end up selling out of fear somewhere towards the bottom of the cycle, thereby crystallising an actual loss as opposed to merely observing a paper loss.

That is not to say market timing is any more obvious to the professional investor. As I stated earlier, no bells are rung nor flags waved ahead of pivotal times in the economic cycle. When asked where the market is, I always have to apologise for the fact that my crystal ball is currently in the repair shop and thus, I'm not able to offer an opinion. There are plenty of advisers who will tell you where the market is going, but I have yet to find one who has consistently got their predictions right over a number of years. My feeling here is that advisers fall into two camps: those who don't know what the market is going to do and those who don't know that they don't know what the market is going to do. I tend to trust the former over the latter.

So, the bottom line here is, it's not possible to time the market consistently. In fact, as much opportunity is lost by being out of the market when it spikes up as it is by being in it when it spikes down. We just don't hear about the days when the market is panic buying. The media only reports bad news, so we only ever see "Black Friday" and "market-meltdown" type headlines.

There is a simple answer – *time in* not *timing*. Commit and stay invested.

Pound-Cost Averaging

Another way to benefit from market volatility is through regular monthly investments, especially when saving out of your income over the long term. If you set up a regular programme, you won't worry so much about market timing. A regular direct debit just goes out of your account and into the portfolio you've set up. Sure enough, if the market goes down, then you automatically pick up your investments at a low price.

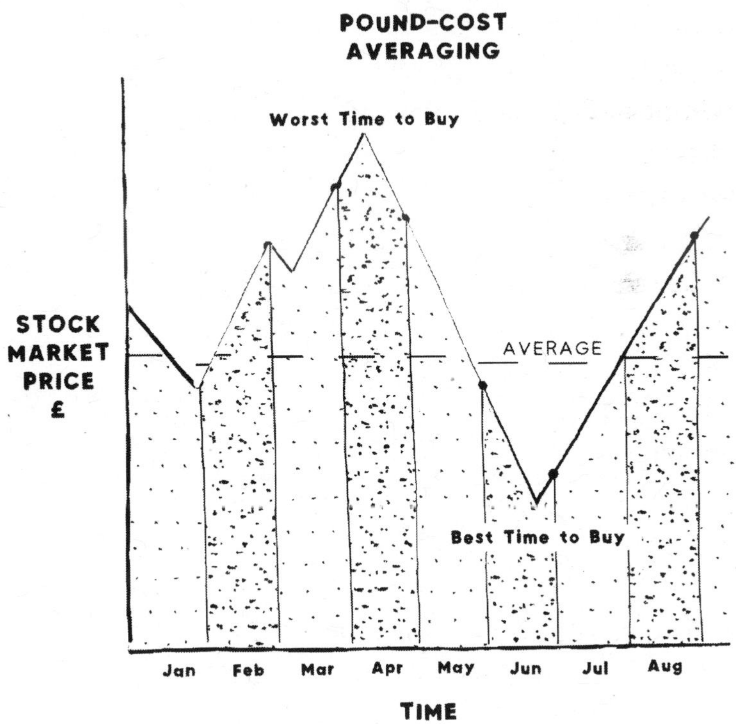

Figure 8

So, when the market goes up, you'll see strong growth on the share you bought cheap. Alternatively, if the market is high, you'll pay a higher price. But over time you'll not only benefit from the discipline of having actually invested, you'll be paying an average or "fair" price. If the market rises over time – which inevitably it does – then you'll reap the rewards. It's a tautology to say if you go ahead and do it, then you can look back and you'll have done it. Whereas, if you don't do it, you won't have done it. But this can be the difference between missing out on building a solid investment portfolio and ending up with nothing, for fear of trying, or trying to perfect the timing. They say the only way to make no mistakes is never to attempt anything; but that, of course, is the biggest mistake of all.

Golden Rules

- Make an income from investments rather than working.
- Save regularly, ideally 10% of your income.
- The eighth wonder of the investment world is compound interest.
- Any money you don't pay tax on increases your net investment return.
- Diversify your investment portfolio across different assets, geographies and risk profiles.

- Insure yourself against adversity (death, critical illness and injury). If you don't get the *time* to create your wealth, then you need the *money* from insurance.

Next, we'll look at how to create wealth.

CHAPTER 8

WEALTH CREATION BASICS AND BUILDING BLOCKS

Who Is This Chapter For?

If you are at the beginning of your financial planning journey, this is for you.

If you want a solid foundation in wealth creation basics, this is for you.

This is also for you if you want to teach your children or grandchildren how to be financially secure and independent (especially the 10% rule!).

The education system in the UK spends much of the curriculum teaching our kids things like differential calculus and the difference between gerunds, participles and infinitives. These aren't particularly helpful life skills in the big wide world. Sadly, what is not included in the basic curriculum are the more practical and fun things like how to forage for food, shelter in the wild, purify water, or how money works.

I remember several years ago when I was doing pro bono teaching at a school just off the Old Kent Road in London, there were some teenagers who were on the cusp of leaving and going out to make their way in the world – super-bright, amazing kids with a massive appetite to learn about the investment world. What shocked me was how little they knew about money. They didn't even understand the difference between a debit and a credit card. We let our kids loose as potential victims to horrific interest rates and confusing debt, completely ill equipped to cope.

It's not surprising there's such a high degree of ignorance around money – it's just not taught at school. So, unless parents understand how money works, and teach their kids the basics of finance, they'll embark on life not knowing any more about money than what they've picked up along the way, which are often unhelpful and misguided beliefs.

It doesn't have to be complicated, but it is important to avoid common traps like not understanding the difference between spending your own money, which doesn't cost you anything, and spending the bank's money on a credit card with as much as a 30% interest rate, which is shocking.

Let's Begin With the Basics

Pay Off High-Interest Debt First

The first thing to do is pay off any expensive debt you've got as soon as you can. If you have expensive credit cards of the 20 or 30% interest variety, it's critical to understand that your money won't earn that sort of return on investment, so it makes sense to use a portion of your income to clear the debt as soon as possible. That way, you're not paying a huge amount of interest every month. Use whatever after-tax income you can to pay off that debt as a priority, and pay off new purchases on high-interest credit cards each month before the interest charge kicks in. Otherwise, that debt will grow fast, and you'll be paying interest on interest (the operation of compound interest with a ruinously negative consequence). No investment stands a chance of competing with the impact of high-cost debt, so don't even think about savings until it's paid off.

Create an Emergency Fund

It's also a good idea to create an emergency fund, which for most people would typically be three to six months' worth of expenditure in a readily accessible bank account. This would cover unforeseen emergency situations such as losing your job, sickness, emergency property repairs or an important medical issue.

Create a Future Financial Security Fund

After you've organised the basics above, I recommend you carve off some income to set aside for your future financial security. It's widely acknowledged good practice to save 10% of your income throughout your working career and invest it. That will be more than adequate to create financial security and I have found that to be true. 20% absolutely guarantees financial comfort. Another popular tip, which used to be a rule of thumb, is to take your age and divide it by two. That gives you the percentage of your income you need to save towards a comfortable retirement. Let's say you're 40 years of age. You would then save 20% in this scenario.

There's some truth in it, but it gets more challenging, the older you get. If you want to retire at 65 and you're already 55, then you've only got 120 monthly pay days left to save for the rest of your life, which puts things into perspective. Using the popular tip, you would need to save around 27% of your income, which may be extremely challenging (and also not enough, so by this stage the rule of thumb fails). The earlier you start, the better, which is why it's so helpful to teach this to your children.

Let's look at the building blocks to creating wealth quickly. Many things in life are *simple*, but not necessarily *easy* – like asking for a date or losing weight. A sensible savings strategy is similarly challenging: the theory is simple, but it requires resolve and action to achieve results. Beyond this discipline, creating wealth will involve getting a decent growth on your money. A good way to maximise this is to ensure you don't pay unnecessary taxes on your investment returns and you make the most of any tax relief the government gives away to encourage savings. This is where an understanding of the basic building blocks of wealth creation is helpful. These blocks tend to be "pots" or "wrappers", which have associated tax benefits that give them optimal utility.

Building Blocks to Creating Wealth

Number 1: Pension

Why is it number 1? Well, it's the only mainstream investment where you get money back from the government to help you towards your savings goals. The government will contribute 20, 40, 45, or even 60% or more, of the contribution you make, based on current tax rates on your level of income. You've got the opportunity to get back some of the national insurance you've paid to the extent that you may only pay one in every three pounds of the contribution. This is the only buy one, get one free in the financial world. Several of my clients have been receiving roughly a 50% tax relief for many years on their pension contributions. Individuals can contribute to pensions but so can limited companies – either way, think of pension contributions as a tax-deductible trading expense. They reduce taxable profit or taxable earnings and allow you to keep all the money you have earned and contributed to a pension rather than giving some of it away.

Over and above tax relief, there are other reasons to invest in a pension:

- The investment return you make will grow free of capital gains and income tax.
- A pension fund is creditor proof in the unfortunate event you go bankrupt. Creditors can't access it.

- And nor can you! You can't get hold of it until later in life, so it keeps the fund safe from the temptation of being spent on something shiny in your younger years.
- You'll receive a tax-free tax sum at the end of your career for your efforts.
- A pension fund is also free of inheritance tax.

You will pay some income tax when you draw money out of your pension fund, but it will usually be considerably less than the tax relief you benefited from on paying the money in. There is no maximum pension pot size but you will only get tax-free cash up to the first £1M or so (at the time of writing).

Now we're going to talk numbers. It's difficult to generalise how much to invest in a pension. It's usually bookended on the one hand by how much you or your business can afford, and by the maximum annual allowance of £60,000 per annum at the other. It's always useful to seek professional advice for your unique situation, but you could regard £1 million as an optimal target. So, with £1 million in a pension fund, let's look at how that might play out.

Personal pensions can be accessed from ten years earlier than the state pension age, so currently age 57. A quarter of the pot can be taken as tax-free cash and the other three-quarters must be used to provide an income, either an annuity or drawing directly from the pot. There is the misconception that a pension pot has to be taken in one go – it doesn't. You can keep it invested and draw little bits regularly or on an ad hoc basis if you prefer.

The way I think of this is as a pie chart, with a quarter of the pie as tax-free cash, and the other three-quarters as taxable. If we imagine each part of the pie as having a "tap" on it that we can turn on or off, or up or down, as we wish, then that's how pension fund proceeds can be drawn out.

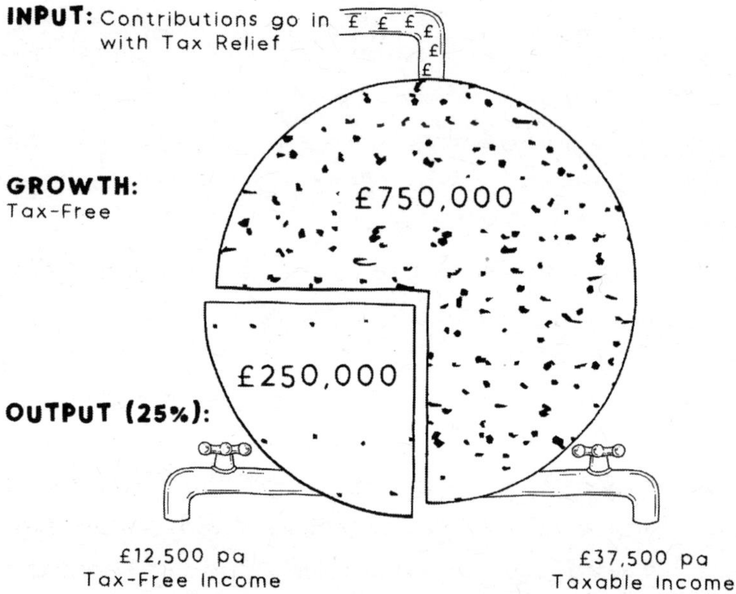

Figure 9

Let's assume we can get a 5% sustainable growth rate on that money. On a £1 million fund value, that's going to throw off around £50,000 per annum as a potential income without depleting the pot. So, a quarter of that would be £12,500 return every year from the tax-free portion.

From the tap on the other three-quarters of the pension pot that is potentially taxable income, at 5% interest, is a return of £37,500 a year. Some of that is going to fall within the Personal Allowance for income tax purposes and can also be tax-free. Assuming the full Personal Allowance is available, that's another £12,500 tax-free. That leaves the remaining £25,000, around half of the total withdrawal, which would be subject to 20% income tax. With half taxed at 20%, we might say that's an aggregate tax rate of 10% on the total income withdrawn, which would be £5,000 tax payable per year, whereas you would have had at least 20% tax relief when paying in, and possibly considerably more than that.

Pensions are *seriously* tax-efficient – especially for higher-rate earners.

Number 2: Individual Savings Account (ISA)

In this case, we're not talking about a regular bank account-based cash ISA because the rates of interest are generally too low and struggle to keep up with inflation. For wealth creation, we're talking about the stocks and shares ISA. This is one for money that you've already paid tax on; you might have inherited money, or it could be the proceeds of the sale of a business or other asset. Any investment into this ISA is going to grow free of both capital gains and income tax. You can cash it in whenever you want but, more importantly, you can take a tax-free income from it. The input level into ISAs is quite generous – in the 2023/24 tax year, it's

£20,000 per person per year. Let's say you're investing this full amount over 15 to 20 years with a half-decent growth rate. You can realistically expect to create an ISA pot of £500,000. Again, using our tax-free withdrawal rate of 5%, it's entirely feasible that it would allow a tax-free income of £25,000 a year. And if you are one of a couple, then you could double that.

Already, you can see there is scope simply from pensions and ISAs to create a reasonably substantial tax-efficient income from a portfolio that is also tax-efficient in terms of growth taxation.

Number 3: General Investment Account (GIA)

The last of the mainstream building blocks is a General Investment Account (GIA), an investment that's not tax wrapped. GIAs take advantage of the general tax allowances available to individuals in terms of investment income and capital gains. It could be a portfolio of individual stocks and shares. It could be a unit trust. It could be an open-ended investment company, which would allow you to take advantage of the dividend income tax-free allowance and the annual capital gains tax exemption. The Autumn Statement in 2022 curbed the capital gains and dividend income allowances, but a GIA is likely a good bet, at least for the time being.

Let's imagine you have £250,000 in a general investment account with a reasonably high growth rate and low dividend. If it achieved a result where the whole 5% return was tax-free, because it used the capital gains tax exemption and the dividend income tax exemption, that would give you another £250,000 working in an effectively tax-free way and generate a further £12,500 a year in tax-free income.

Now let's pause at this point and assume over a lifetime you've been able to fund these three basic structures at optimal levels. You've got an income of £50,000 a year from the pension, £25,000 a year from the ISA and £12,500 from the general investment account, which is a grand total of £87,500 a year. Out of that you will only pay about £5,000 in tax, which is the bit of the pension that strays into the basic rate tax bracket, so, minus that £5,000, you're left with a net income of £82,500. This is a very low tax rate and obviously you will need to pay any tax due as you fund these structures. You can see in these examples how proper planning and use of the allowance of these structures over time leads to high levels of tax-light income in later life.

How Big a Pot Can I Get? The Variables

The variables are the term over which you save, the investment return that you receive and above all how much you put in. These variables are determined by your age, the amount of disposable income you invest and how well your investments perform.

It tends to be the case that people start off small and, if their career takes a typical route, they earn more money as their experience develops. Your expenses might increase if you have a family, but then eventually you'll end up with an excess investible income. You only put in what you can afford to put in, but the major building blocks towards creating a wealth pot you can draw on in later life are pensions, ISAs and GIAs, in that order.

When Should You Pay Off Your Mortgage?

Paying off your mortgage is another way of accumulating more wealth and is a desirable thing to do. I don't recommend paying off your mortgage as the priority, though, if it means not having any money in the aforementioned tax-advantaged pots. With the input levels to pensions and ISAs, it's a case of "use it or lose it". If you pay off your mortgage over many, many years without building up pensions and ISAs, then you are restricted as to how much can go in in later life – and you may run out of time. This is where a financial planning professional comes in handy because they help prioritise what is the most efficient fund to create first and how much to invest.

Advanced Wealth Creation

There are other investments, beyond the scope of this book, which would apply to people who've already accumulated a large amount of wealth, sold a business or received an inheritance and have substantial capital assets they want to preserve. Typically, the next steps would be vehicles like investment bonds and family investment companies, which can help preserve wealth. They offer opportunities to avoid inheritance tax and pass assets onto future generations or create a legacy.

Also beyond the aim of this book, but good to know for getting tax relief on investments, are venture capital trusts and enterprise investment schemes. These are for more sophisticated investors with a very high tolerance to risk, but with very tax-favoured status to get more money back from the government. They create tax-free growth and income, and are very positive for impact investment because they can be targeted at companies developing and offering services to address social and environmental issues.

Assets Versus Liabilities

Let's wrap up this chapter with an important point: understanding the difference between an asset and a liability. I frequently have interesting conversations with clients about investing in holiday homes, which seems like an attractive opportunity. A holiday home can be an asset, but be careful because it could soon switch to being a liability if it's expensive to run. Your property is likely to need at least some of the following, which all come at a cost: management, repairs, refurbishments, gardeners, air conditioning and heating, council tax, service charges, insurance and regular cleaning, which can quickly drain your profits, especially if it isn't easy to let.

When you have created wealth, the next step is to preserve it.

CHAPTER 9

WEALTH PRESERVATION

In Chapters 7 and 8, we looked at some common-sense basics of accumulating wealth, and which structures should be in place to make sure your wealth doesn't end up burdened by tax.

In Chapter 9, we're going to concentrate on wealth preservation. If we consider the previous stage as being the accumulation phase of savings, or the working phase of one's life, then this is the retirement stage. And within that, we might also view it as legacy planning. Of course, your wealth might not have come to you through the accumulation phase. You might have inherited it. It might be from the sale of a business. It could be a family legacy or the proceeds of a property sale or downsize.

As I mentioned earlier, people can feel anxious about how to preserve their capital, and how to maintain their desired lifestyle with their funds. With this in mind, we will spend some time thinking about the important aspects of how to preserve wealth and, potentially, pass it on, but certainly how to use it in such a way that you can enjoy the life you want to have, funded by that money.

At the start of Part Two, we looked at the four variables that determine the answer to how much is enough. While they are important in working out how much you need to accumulate and when you can consider yourself financially independent, they are equally vital for working out how you need to preserve your capital. As a reminder, the variables are:

- How much do you intend to spend every year of the rest of your life?
- How long are you going to live?
- What investment return will you get?
- What will the rate of inflation be?

Let's concentrate on these in a little more detail with reference to wealth preservation.

Budget

You need a budget to decide how much income you want to take from your investments. This will be a key driver in figuring out how much you need to invest (or accumulate) in order to fulfil your life goals. You might also have to determine how much to keep if you want to give money away to family and/or philanthropically if you have “too much”. This is very difficult to predict. Current expenditure is probably quite easy to pin down with careful analysis. Experience tells me most people vastly underestimate this if they don’t carry out careful analysis. The future is harder to predict. It may be the case that expenditure even goes up in early retirement and then down as we slow down. Or, equally well, expenditure may go down in early retirement when your kids and your mortgage are less of a drain, but then go up vastly in late retirement, with private care home costs. For the much wealthier clients – how much is to be put into a trust for future generations and what will they need?

Timeline

The length of time available to invest will inform the risk you can afford to take. If there’s a short-term spending aim, for example, you probably don’t want to expose your money to volatility in case it goes down. If you’re relatively young and healthy, and expect a long life, then you can afford to take relatively high degrees of risk. This is the case in particular if you’re investing for legacy planning for children or grandchildren; the timeline for that could be very, very long. The advantage of having a long investment timeline is that any fall in the value of your investments, whilst unwelcome, only becomes real if you’re forced to sell. But when you’ve got time on your side, you’re able to ride out any downturns or a recession, to allow the investment the possibility of recovering in value.

If you anticipate many more years of earned income, then this indicates a higher capacity for risk, since losses can be made up out of income. But if you don't have the capacity for earned income, then it becomes even more important to preserve your capital.

It's also important to consider your natural attitude towards investment risk. Some people are comfortable seeing their investments go up and down as markets go through their different stages; other people less so. An appropriate portfolio would be mapped to your personal attitude to investment risk. And it's worth having professional counselling around what your appropriate risk level should be, taking your natural attitude to risk into account, but also the other key factors.

We've talked about how shorter-term investments should be safer and longer-term investments more volatile. That means an investment portfolio should be designed with the asset allocation carefully in mind. Studies show that asset allocation is one of the biggest predictors to the success of an investment portfolio. We might say that a typical portfolio for a balanced investor comprises 50 to 70% invested in stocks and shares, with 30 to 50% in so-called safer assets, such as cash, fixed interest bonds and possibly property. The more risk-averse, the higher the risk investment would be. And how long the timeline, and how speculative the investor is, determines the best equities or assets.

Your Investment Risk

Let's consider real assets and investment again. We've looked at bank accounts and how the capital value won't go down. Cash might appear to be a risk-free asset, but, as we've seen, its relative purchasing power can go down, so it's important to think in terms of what risk is. There's even risk in not taking risk. I think that is a smart way of reframing our expectations for investments in order to achieve a positive rate of return. You can't achieve it without exposing yourself to some risk. Risk can be difficult to define because tolerance levels vary from person to person depending on their attitudes and circumstances.

In any field of endeavour, we must push the boundaries into the unknown to create opportunity. The bigger the risk, the bigger the opportunity, but so too is the corresponding risk of loss. There are legitimate fears about stepping away from the "safe" zone and onto the risk spectrum. There's the fear of incurring loss, and it's inevitable there will be some degree of volatility beyond that. Profits can be made, but the inexperienced investor may fear being taken advantage of, and making costly mistakes.

Paradoxically, staying safe also carries risk and can be an even bigger mistake. Timid naivety usually ends in tears when it turns out that what appeared safe was, in fact, not safe at all. And with investments, that could be high inflation, it could be a banking crisis, or it could even be fraud. It's best to confront the inevitable and accept risk as an inescapable part of investment, just as it is in life. Most investors understand they've got to take some risk to have the best chance of achieving their financial goals. Moving away from the realm of safety and into the realm of risk is where opportunity and progress are, and with a wise guide and some sensible principles, you can get the balance right between risk and reward.

If you're only investing a small amount of your liquid capital, you can afford to take relatively larger risks. For a portfolio that represents more of your wealth, a more cautious approach will typically be necessary, with safer assets for the shorter term, a more balanced portfolio for the medium term, and potentially higher risk for long-term investment.

What is Inflation?

For anybody under the age of 40, inflation won't have really been much of a feature of life. It's been benign for the last 20 years, but for people who remember the 1970s and 1980s, inflation was problematic. 2022 saw inflation come roaring back to life, catching out fund managers and affecting mortgage payers, who are facing steep increases in mortgage payments on top of the prices of essentials including electricity.

In basic terms, inflation is the price of things going up. It's critical our money keeps pace with inflation, because if it doesn't, our purchasing power plummets. There are only a couple of ways to protect our investments against inflation. The first one is investing in what I call "real assets". Real assets are typically those that give an income. The most obvious one is property. A property is a great hedge against inflation.

You would hope that your property would rise in value over time, as property historically has done in the UK. When inflation goes up, it pushes the price of things and the cost of living up, including house prices. Owning an additional property (not the one you live in) would combat inflation to some extent and the rental yield would typically go up and down in line with inflation pressures, as demand and supply balance out in the marketplace. That's one example of an asset which should keep pace with inflation to some extent.

The other way to protect your investments against inflation is through stocks and shares. We talked before about how stocks and shares go up and down in value and how the dividend can be viewed like the rental yield on a property. Companies and shares are extremely dynamic over time. Although the prospect of inflation can depress share prices in the short term, it's different for the longer term. In the long run, if businesses react to the need to keep making a profit, their shares are likely to keep pace with inflation.

Of course, any invested asset brings with it a degree of risk. Indeed, the only way to avoid risk with assets that might fluctuate in value is to leave money in a cash bank account. Cash in a bank won't go down unless the banker goes bust. While a bank balance will never go down in absolute terms, it can go down in relative terms. If your bank account's paying you a 1% interest rate, and inflation is running at 6%, then the price of stuff is going up at 6%. If your money's only going up at 1%, it's losing 5% in relative terms.

Inflation is catastrophic for savers. Leaving money in assets which cannot keep pace with the rate of inflation will erode its purchasing power. Furthermore, and rather ironically, inflation leads to more inflation as wages have to react to increasing prices. This damaging feedback loop for savers is something governments thought they had a handle on.

Where it's catastrophic for savers, inflation is potentially quite useful for borrowers. Let's say you've got debt – a mortgage on a property you bought. The amount of the debt is fixed, so it doesn't go up regardless of what inflation is doing. But inflation will be driving up the value of the property and also driving up your income. Thus, your mortgage gets smaller in two ways:

- The repayments become a smaller percentage of your income since your income's gone up, but your mortgage repayments haven't (assuming a fixed rate mortgage).
- The debt as a percentage of the property value goes down.

Other big borrowers relate to sovereign debt. We talked about fixed interest earlier, where borrowers such as governments pay a set rate of interest for the duration of their loan. Governments have been able to issue bonds over very long terms, fixed at exceptionally low rates over the past few years. By the same principle, a practical, if cynical, way for governments to reduce debt in real terms would be to engineer a healthy dose of inflation into the economy. So, inflation can be useful for those with high levels of debt (and who can use fiscal and macro-economic levers to attain such a goal). 2022 saw the advent of inflation not so much creeping back as storming back. 'Be careful what you wish for!' is the maxim of the law of unintended consequences. About a fifth of UK debt is still linked to the old Retail Price Index (RPI) measure of inflation. That means the government could soon be facing double-digit interest rates on a significant portion of its debt (about half a trillion pounds). That's what I would refer to, technically, as "a chunk of change" – and it won't be a comfortable place to be. Getting the inflation genie back in the bottle is usually a very hard trick to pull off.

Bringing it All Together: Managing Your Money and Creating a Financial Plan

We have established that there are many variables and risks. Here's a summary:

- Living too long
- Dying too soon
- Getting sick
- How much is enough?

- How do we instil values in the kids around money?
- How can I pass on my wealth?
- How long will I live?
- What will my expenditure needs be over the course of my lifetime?
- What might inflation be?
- What investment return will I get?
- Knowing what tax wrappers exist, and optimal use
- Protection and life assurance
- Your attitude to investment risk
- Risk assessment of investments
- Designing an optimal asset allocation
- Stock and fund selection
- Ongoing portfolio management

Working with an experienced financial planner helps with all of the above areas; someone skilful who's not afraid to confront the difficult questions and conversations that lead to better outcomes. They'll often also pay for their fees from tax savings, superior investment performance or simply peace of mind that these factors have been taken into account. According to Investopedia, taking professional advice can lead to much better financial outcomes.[20] In one study by Morningstar, good financial decisions resulted in a

20 https://www.investopedia.com/articles/personal-finance/102616/how-much-can-advisor-help-your-returns-how-about-3-worth.asp

29% higher retirement income. This is the equivalent of about 2% per year of additional returns after charges. Vanguard put the additional return from taking advice at nearer 3%.

Whatever way you go about it, there still remains the question of how to manage the actual money. Most people don't have the time, energy, or the skill to find the best individual stocks to suit their needs. And even if they do, the dealing costs associated with trading stocks and shares are quite high and you need a big number of holdings to achieve adequate diversification, which wouldn't just be across different industries but across different geographies as well. Investors in the UK are familiar with the FTSE 100 stocks, or the hundred biggest companies in the UK, but limiting investment to just this presents two serious problems. One is that it doesn't give you much diversification, i.e. it lacks exposure to other geographies and currencies or small to medium-sized companies. The other is that the FTSE 100 is a "dirty" index from the point of view of ethical values, people and the planet. A third of that index comprises companies which are negative within impact investment – fossil fuel companies, the banks that lend to them, tobacco companies and mining companies. Therefore, most investors will choose funds to get exposure to the asset classes with a well-diversified range of stocks and shares.

As if investment wasn't hard enough when choosing what funds are likely to perform better, there's the additional layer of research needed for successful impact investment. In the UK, there are over 8,000 investment funds, which is an enormous selection to get your head around. As you can imagine, you need to do a lot of research to figure out which ones to buy and it can be extremely difficult and time-consuming. This is the benefit of working with someone who puts together an investment management methodology, which will lead to suitable balance from a risk perspective and consider your unique position and ethical values.

Finally, there is the age-old argument of whether a cheap, passive approach is better than a more expensive, active approach. The adviser or fund house that prefers cheap passive will argue that the money saved in charges will translate to superior investment returns over time, thus you can trust a programmatic asset-allocation strategy. A good, active fund manager on the other hand will argue that buying better stocks and avoiding bad ones will outperform costly research and outweigh the inevitable additional charges that come with a more intensive research process.

While the investor and the financial advisory community can debate these pros and cons until the cows come home, there is one inescapable fact when it comes to impact investment: programmatic index-based passive funds are not at all rigorous in terms of ESG and impact assessment. So, to my mind, if you want to be sure all nuances have been properly researched, then you're stuck with the more expensive, active funds. Much like organic vegetables or fair trade coffee, ethics come at a price.

In the next chapter, we will look at investment risk in more detail.

CHAPTER 10

RISK AND REWARD

We've talked about financial planning strategy and investment timelines. Now we'll look at successful investment strategy because a successful investment strategy is crucial to your financial well-being. It's got to have the potential to increase your wealth and prosperity, and so it has to achieve a positive return and one that substantially outpaces increases in the cost of living over the longer term. You cannot achieve this without exposing yourself to risk.

The Six Key Areas of Risk

The six key areas to take into account for your attitude to investment and tolerance risk are:

1. **Time horizon**
   Generally, the shorter the period you have available to invest, the lower the risk you can afford to take. If you have a longer timeline, you can afford to take

more risk, since you might have to wait for a falling investment to recover from short-term loss. The loss only becomes real when you're forced to sell, and that only happens if you're too uncomfortable to ride out the storm, or if you need to access the money while the price is low.

2. **Investment amount**
   If you're investing small amounts of your liquid capital, then you can afford to take relatively larger risks. With a portfolio, however, which represents more of your wealth, it would be prudent to have a more balanced or cautious approach.

3. **Your income**
   Many more years of earned income would indicate a higher capacity for risk since you can make losses up out of future income. If earning capacity is very limited, risk appetite can be reduced.

4. **Your objectives**
   Some investments are made to achieve income whereas others are to target capital growth. Some investments have quite secure income streams, even though the capital value might be more volatile. Different investment behaviours and risks may vary from one objective to another. Overall balance will be the key.

5. **Stage of life and frequency of investments**
   If you're young and making monthly investments, I recommend you welcome high risk and volatility,

with an attitude of less to lose and a greater capacity for loss. Buying the market at different price points means that sometimes you'll buy cheap and other times high, but you'll pay the average price over the longer term.

6. **Your natural attitude to risk**
   A lot of people would list natural attitude to risk the number one factor, but all the other factors need to be considered first. If you're of a more cautious disposition, you might be uncomfortable watching your investments go up and down, especially if the movement is substantial. Therefore, even if you have a high capacity for loss, I recommend you don't do anything that makes you too nervous. Conversely, if you've got a higher capacity for loss and you embrace investment risk, you might well prefer a more adventurous approach.

Besides personal risk factors, there are certain systemic investment risk factors:

Your investments could fall in value

Almost all investments can fall in value. Supply and demand, confidence, regulatory, political influence, governance, obsolescence, interest rates – all these potential risks need to be assessed and their relevance given an appropriate rating.

Inflation in general

Your actual cash value might not go down but lower-risk investments have lower returns. Your spending power could suffer if inflation is higher than your investment return.

Liquidity: avoid the situation where you are forced to sell

If prices are depressed, it's vital you hold sufficient cash so that you can wait out times of lower prices. A well-diversified portfolio will have lower risk and higher risk elements. It's important these elements are held discretely so that you can sell the lower-risk ones whilst hanging on to the higher-risk ones and waiting for the recovery.

Lack of diversification

If your investments all correlate and behave similarly at the same time, you have a very unbalanced portfolio. Being better diversified avoids putting all of your eggs in one basket and gives you a chance to continue to make investment returns from your portfolio. An example of negative correlation might be umbrellas and ice cream – typically, sales of one will be higher when the other are lower. This is an example of a better-diversified portfolio than umbrellas and Wellington boots.

An investor considering a "green" portfolio might worry that it won't be sufficiently well diversified. Most investment areas can still be accessed with what we call an "impact" portfolio. Admittedly, the portfolio won't be investing in, say, fossil fuels or tobacco, but that doesn't mean you can't be invested in power or health outcomes. It'll just be renewable energy and healthcare, as opposed to poisonous gas and toxins.

A lack of review process

Fund managers change regularly. The chances of a fund manager being fired, promoted, headhunted or retiring are very high. How do you keep tabs on these movements and how do you decide whether to stick with the fund house or follow the fund manager if they move? Unless you have a regular review, rebalance your investments, and consider threats and opportunities from time to time, your portfolio can become dated and vulnerable. And not only that, your priorities, goals and timeline may change.

Stranded assets

A company's balance sheet value will be predicated on its ability to exploit all the assets it owns. If the planet is to have any chance of achieving its agreed emission targets, then oil companies have no choice but to leave a vast amount of their reserves in the ground. They could face rapid and negative revaluation. Other examples of possible stranded assets include car manufacturing and tooling. And changes in consumer behaviour or legislation could have a profound and abrupt destabilising effect on prices.

All these risks may mean you can't get back as much as you invest. A good investment management process will consider these personal and systemic risk factors. With a sensible financial plan and understanding the tax structures, you should be able to decide what's right for you in your unique situation and be able to frame risk to help you understand the context more fully. Too little risk is as bad as too much risk.

Lack of adaptability

Let's look at where good inflation-proof returns come from. Many sources have quoted the statistic that £1 invested in the year 1900 would be worth approximately £30,000 today. Even allowing for inflation, that's a stunning real rate of return. The non-inflation adjusted number is something ridiculous, like £2.5 million. Clearly, savers should be investing in becoming dynamic and creative entrepreneurs. Sharing in risk entitles investors to share in the profits, and, as we can see, the profits can be very large. Forward-thinking businesspeople will adapt and change their products, services and processes accordingly. And changing the world, disrupting, and introducing their business visions may require more investment. Without stocks and shares as investible assets, much of that progress would be slower or not realised at all.

Stocks and shares are arguably the only financial assets capable of truly creating a transformational shift in wealth. For the long haul, equities give higher returns. A good equity investment gives you a stake in a business, which will ideally be managed by competent people with good governance and who can react quickly to changing trends, consumer tastes and the prevailing economic environment. We think of this "stake" as part ownership of a real business run by real people trying to create real solutions for real customer problems and needs. It's one of the real assets we talked about earlier, and it's the beauty of the capitalist model in action, where capital ventured can participate with enthusiastic entrepreneurs to create wealth.

Designing Your Investment Portfolio

In my experience, the best possible portfolio investments – for reasons of simplicity – are equities, bonds and cash. Please refer to the table below for the advantages and risks of each asset class.

We might rank an investment risk on a scale of 1 to 10, where 1 is very cautious and 10 is very adventurous. Broadly, risk 1 would be 10% equities and 90% bonds, meaning only 10% of the portfolio would be exposed to high volatility and risk. 90% would be safe. Risk 2 would be 20% equities and 80% bonds. Risk 3 would be 30% equities and 70% bonds, and so on, through to an adventurous, possibly high-risk, portfolio. At the extreme end of the scale, risk 10 would be 100% equities and 0% bonds.

From a universe comprised of 8,000 funds, how do you construct a well-diversified portfolio across different geographical industries and company sizes, as well as differentiate between companies which have growth prospects and those which are income-producing?

INVESTMENT TYPE	ADVANTAGES	RISKS
Cash/Bank deposits	▸ Very low chance of direct loss ▸ Not volatile	▸ Very low return ▸ Unlikely to keep pace with inflation
Government Bonds (Also know as gilts – comprise a loan to the government with a fixed return over a fixed term)	▸ Typically better return than cash ▸ Known (fixed) return ▸ Return virtually guaranteed since very low default risk ▸ Capital returned on maturity	▸ Low return ▸ Longer-dated bonds will be affected by interest rate movements
Corporate Bonds (Comprise a loan to a company with a fixed return over a fixed term)	▸ Typically better return than gilts ▸ Known return ▸ Wide range of risk options ▸ Capital returned on maturity	▸ Higher risk than gilts since issuing company more likely to default ▸ Prices affected by sentiment and the economy generally as well as interest rates
Equities (Owning shares in a company to generate dividents and hoped-for capital appreciation)	▸ Higher returns over the medium to longer term ▸ Dividends tend to be very stable	▸ Volatile ▸ Performance depends on many factors
Residential Property	▸ Easily understood ▸ Good hedge against inflation	▸ Very high maintenance ▸ Liquidity can be a problem ▸ Void periods ▸ Quality of income (tenant)
Commercial Property	▸ Higher potential quality of tenant and hence guaranteed income ▸ Tenant 'on the hook' for long leases ▸ Wider diversification ▸ Assets can potentially be improved	▸ High unit size ▸ Macro-economic risk (e.g. retail and threat from online) ▸ Tenants can go bust or demand landlord takes a 'haircut'
Alternative Assets (Gold, timber, hedge funds, crypto)	▸ Negative correlation for other assets possible ▸ Reduced volatility	▸ Less well understood ▸ Often sluggish performance ▸ Often higher risk ▸ Leverage will increase risk

Figure 10

There are various approaches to constructing a balanced portfolio. One might be to choose a managed fund or a fund of funds from a typical product provider. You might engage with a model portfolio service – a bit like a football squad with its turnover of players – which introduces new funds and gets rid of old ones over time. You could appoint your own investment manager. You might manage your stocks yourself or choose very cheap tracker funds. Research concludes that asset allocation is the most important long-term predictor of financial success.

There's also the choice between passive and active investment management. Passive is very cheap and follows various indices and trackers. It's not a method I engage with because the sustainability and research are not rigorous enough, so I work with active fund managers who can outperform the market.

It's important to choose an investment platform which gives you access to every fund in the fund universe. Other elements to consider are whether you buy in separate analytical research, whether you work with an independent financial adviser, who takes an overview of the entire picture, and which investment managers make up the portfolio.

These are the components of a modular architecture of fund design, for creating a dynamic and adaptable management style where any aspect of the process can be changed as the need arises or as better options evolve.

CONCLUSION

THE CHOICE IS OURS

How Much Capital is There in the World to Make a Difference with?

Let's consider the total invested capital in the world. Estimates vary on how much free investible capital there is, but most hover around the $200 trillion mark. The International Finance Corporation (IFC), a division of the World Bank Group, talks about the fact that availability of information on measured impact assets has increased and there are certain operating principles for impact management, in terms of ESG measures, that make up about half of the impact assets under management. They say there is an increasing level of transparency and discipline in the market.

An IFC report identifies assets that can be credibly observed to be managed with intent for positive impact and have an identifiable contribution and a measurement of impact.[21] Taking these three measures, the IFC estimate $363 billion of assets come under the measured impact definition. The Global Impact Investing Network (GIIN) estimate is higher at $715 billion, as of 2020, which is up from $502 billion in 2019. These are the assets that could be considered having a measurable impact.

There's another slice of assets, valued at $1,646 billion, that appears to fulfil measurements one and two: they've got intent and there's a credible narrative, but they're not yet fully measurable. This means that somewhere in the region of over $2 trillion, out of the total market of about $200 trillion, fits the definition of impact investment. Impact investment is growing fast, but it's still relatively tiny. Early adopters can aspire to reap the benefits. There's a long way to go, as the market adopts to what we would define impact investment, but as much as $50 trillion is now judged as having some type of ESG credential. ESG is emerging as the new normal, and impact investment is still some way behind, but likely to grow massively.

We find ourselves in a world where rising temperatures are making parts of the world uninhabitable. Climate change and increased rainfall are causing flooding, and food and water shortage, much of which is induced by the Anthropocene impact.

We find ourselves at a time where, more than ever before, money is a force with the power to alter

21 https://www.ifc.org/wps/wcm/connect/corp_ext_content/ifc_external_corporate_site/annual+report/download

our future. These issues must be addressed, and it's essential we reduce the amount of carbon emissions in the atmosphere. There are sufficient resources to feed the entire population of the world, but we need to spur systemic change. And invested capital can fuel this transformative innovation.

You are reading this book because you have vision and foresight – and you can be part of changing the way we look at investing. When I had my epiphany, I set up a company which was unashamedly for profit because capitalism is the force that drives change. Money follows money, and money creates the momentum to make positive change. It has to be this way, otherwise we'll be forced to continue to rely on the wealthy to be philanthropic. We live in hope that governments will do things that aren't natural for them to want to do, with their short-term view. Companies continue to be short-termist in their attitudes, and so we find ourselves at a tipping point, as Malcolm Gladwell might say.

There's enough momentum now through campaigners such as Leonardo DiCaprio and organisations such as Make My Money Matter, Good Money, and the Good Egg Award to democratise capital and make people aware of the influence they can have through their financial decisions. We're shining a light on what is a bit of an abstract black box. This is a call to action for consumers, the financial advisory community, fund managers and companies to think about how they act. This was an area dominated by universities and faith groups. But this growing awareness gives individuals the power to move their money so it aligns with their values.

> **There's no such thing as a neutral investment. Every investment has an impact.**

We have more compelling evidence of the financial success of impact investment and we're seeing the emergence of stranded assets, where their value is tied up in a way that will never be realised. Thus, we are on the path to a new normal, where the future is not just a screenout of Environmental, Social and Governance "nasties" but one where impact is integrated into all financial decisions. Impact investment is the key. People will have the opportunity to align their money with their values, and a more granular measurement will emerge.

Fintech will allow further empowerment of wealth, as things like voting tools are integrated onto financial platforms so that consumers understand the stocks and shares they invest in and are able to cast their vote at AGMs in a way they currently can't because of the black box nature of investment.

We are at a monumental crossroads in history. There's a wealth transfer to women and to younger generations, who, as a sweeping generality, are more inclined to be mindful about the way their money behaves, which will help speed up the transition.

Impact investment is aligned with scarcity and inflation. In the past, when it was scarce, oil was an investment which did very well. Looking to the future, innovations in food and water will be excellent investments, as will green infrastructure and carbon capture. I see this as a virtuous circle, where profit will be derived from doing the *right* thing, and through money dictating behavioural change. That's where conscious investors will find profit.

So, in conclusion, with everything else being equal, we must ask ourselves whether we are happy killing the planet with our money, or whether we are going to act, and choose to save the planet with our money.

The choice is ours ...

ACKNOWLEDGEMENTS

Thanks to Rachel Henke for her support in helping write this book. Her patience in getting the material out of my head and down onto paper was no mean achievement. It's safe to say that without her encouragement and skill it's unlikely this book would have materialised!

Thanks also to the rest of the publishing team: proof-editor Yasmin Yarwood, typesetter Catherine Williams and illustrator Gary Nightingale. Your enthusiasm, professionalism and output has been amazing.

I'd also like to thank all of the team at Path Financial for their support.

And Tara and my kids for their love and inspiration throughout.